*55 FAST TIPS
to Jump-start *Your*
Real Estate Business

SELLING
Simplified

Michelle Moore

Managing Editor: Alice Sullivan, www.alicesullivan.com

First and foremost, I want to thank my Lord and Savior, Jesus Christ,
for entrusting me with the knowledge contained in this book.

This book is dedicated to my loving husband, Jeff.
Thank you for faithfully supporting me in all my
endeavors throughout our years together.

A special thank you to Elaine Shaneyfelt, Christy Kirchner,
Dina Miller, Karen Robinson, Barbara Gibbons, Jackie Alexander,
Jillian Chambers, Sharon Hamilton, Sandy Powell, Cindy Rushton,
and Angela Williams—godly women who inspired, elevated,
believed, encouraged, and challenged me to answer the call on my
life to make a difference in the lives of others. Thank you also to
John Kirchner for always speaking life into my dreams and daring
to dream even bigger for me than I can dream for myself, at times.

Contents

Introduction

In a short amount of time, and with very little money, you can have your very own real estate business. Rarely does beginning your business get any faster, cheaper, or easier.

Getting into the new-home sales side of the real estate business early in my career afforded me the unique opportunities to learn, and then practice what I learned. Most weeks I was meeting and working with more prospective buyers than most resale agents get to speak with in an entire month.

Truth be told, the real estate industry is simply set up for failure, for the most part. In real estate classes, you learn a lot of terminology and not much of how to accomplish day-to-day responsibilities of being a Realtor®. Of course, you learn the importance of location and other real estate basics. Most individuals getting into real estate have never owned their own business, been in sales, or even studied marketing. Most have never set goals, planned a budget, or generated leads.

At the time I became interested in real estate, I was a computer programmer. I was tired of making very little money but working very hard to be good at what I did. I began thinking about what else I could do so that my hard work would be reflected by my income. I liked the thought of sales, but my only sales experience was that I had been the top-selling Girl Scout Cookie seller in all of Montgomery County, Tennessee, at age ten. Because of that, I spoke at a Brownie and Girl Scout Convention about goal setting and working hard to meet those goals. Even at a young age, I knew the benefits of preparation and hard work. So when I became interested in real estate, I approached it with tenacity and sought out as much knowledge as I could possibly find. I refused to leave my life's success up to chance, no matter the career. One great piece of knowledge I learned about early on in my career is called The Four Stages of Learning.

THE FOUR STAGES OF LEARNING

The Four Stages of Learning suggests that individuals are initially unaware of how little they know, or are unconscious of their incompetence. As they recognize their incompetence, they consciously acquire a skill. Then, they consciously use that skill. Eventually, the skill can be done without consciously being thought through, and the individual is said to have unconscious competence.

1. UNCONSCIOUS INCOMPETENCE

   The individual does not understand or know how to do something and does not necessarily recognize the deficit. They may deny the usefulness of the skill. The individual must recognize their own incompetence, and the value of the new skill, before moving on to the next stage. The length of time an individual spends in this stage depends on the strength of the stimulus to learn.

2. CONSCIOUS INCOMPETENCE

   Though the individual does not understand or know how to do something, he or she does recognize the deficit, as well as the value of a new skill in addressing the deficit. The making of mistakes can be integral to the learning process at this stage.

3. CONSCIOUS COMPETENCE

   The individual understands or knows how to do something. However, demonstrating the skill or knowledge requires concentration. It may be broken down into steps, and there is heavy conscious involvement in executing the new skill.

4. UNCONSCIOUS COMPETENCE

The individual has had so much practice with a skill that it has become "second nature" and can be performed easily. As a result, the skill can be performed while executing another task. The individual may also be able to teach it to others.

Early on in my real estate career, I made a decision to commit to "self-mastery." Mastery is a decision to excel at something, a decision to put in the time and effort to achieve excellence, and a decision to reject mediocrity and failure. Whether I was reading a training manual on how to sell, or reviewing notes from a trainer about construction terms, I poured over the pages repeatedly.

Through the years, I have spoken with many people who got into the real estate business because they liked looking at houses. However, I found that they seemed to have no idea that looking at or showing real estate—whether residential, land, or commercial—is such a small, small portion of how a real estate professional spends his or her time while conducting business. There's so much more to real estate! And the more you know, the more success you will have. After all, knowledge is power.

The purpose of this book is to:

- Inform: Bring awareness of what you don't know.
- Educate: Learn what, why, where, and how.
- Inspire: You can meet or exceed your goals!

I cover what is needed to obtain a high level of success in real estate and my goal is to help you reach the Unconscious Competence stage in every area of your real estate business. If obtaining a level of excellence in every aspect of your real estate career is at the top of your goal sheet (see Tip 6), you are in the right business.

Whether you are considering getting your real estate license, are new in the real estate business, or you have been selling real estate for over twenty-five years, this book is for you!

Selling Simplified is an indispensable source of information that includes the fifty-five essential tips to successfully sell real estate in any market, in any city, and in any state. These are tips that I learned and have personally used to succeed at an extraordinary level. This book is chock-full of proven and factual tips, tools, and techniques from my real world experiences. And I am sharing them to give you the edge you need to excel in today's competitive real estate business environment. *Selling Simplified* is for anyone who is ready to realize their goals and fulfill their highest potential.

During my time as the CEO/Team Leader for Keller Williams Realty, in Nashville, I realized there was not a current book (similar to what I had read when considering getting into the business over eighteen years ago) that covered much of the day-to-day responsibilities that would lead to experiencing success. It is my hope that this book becomes a resource tool for recruiters, real estate schools, and real estate companies throughout the industry.

Steve Jobs once said, "Be a yardstick of quality. Some people aren't used to an environment where excellence is expected." My challenge to you is this: As you read, learn, and implement the tips throughout this book, be the yardstick of quality in real estate sales. Commit to excellence. Make a commitment to, as I like to say, "Be your top."

The best way to get something done is to begin. So, let's get started.

FAST TIP *1

Correct Your Mindset

"IF YOU THINK YOU CAN OR THINK YOU
CAN'T, YOU'RE RIGHT EITHER WAY."
– Henry Ford

How badly do you want a successful real estate career?

The real estate industry is not an easy business. Somehow the general public believes it's fun, easy, and everyone makes a ton of money. After all, we do add the words "Million-Dollar Producer" to our business cards and various marketing materials, leaving the public to assume we all earn at least a million dollars every year. Even Hollywood makes fun of real estate agents and the horrible stigmas attached to salespeople. Fact is, it is hard work, long hours, and has no glamour included.

Reprogram your self-limiting beliefs about "success." If you believe that success is hard, or that you will have to sacrifice your personal life, or that to be successful you have to be selfish and aggressive, then that is what you will create. The results of holding onto these anti-success beliefs is obvious—you just keep pushing it away day after day, month after month, and year after year. Success seems out of reach. If you do manage to achieve it, you'll push it away.

But here's the good news: It doesn't matter how many years you've had a belief; the power to change that belief is always in the present moment. That's why it's so important to identify the belief and bring it to the surface. First, discover the origins of those self-limiting beliefs and pull them out by the roots, like pulling weeds. Then, replace those self-limiting beliefs with empowered beliefs. For example, "I have a valuable service to offer, and people are happy to hear from me." When you radiate a positive attitude, you are magnetizing what you desire and what you deserve.

Louise L. Hay once said, "Affirmations are like seed planted in soil. Poor soil, poor growth. Rich soil, abundant growth. The more you choose to think thoughts that make you feel good, the quicker the affirmations work." Begin speaking life into yourself and your business today to experience that abundant growth.

BONUS: Visit www.SellingSimplifiedNow.com to receive a FREE copy of *Selling Simplified*'s Ten Positive Affirmations to Speak Daily over Yourself and Your Business.

FAST TIP *2

It's All about Attitude

"YOUR ATTITUDE, NOT YOUR APTITUDE,
WILL DETERMINE YOUR ALTITUDE."
–Zig Ziglar

No one else controls your mind and your attitude unless they have your permission. The same goes for uncomfortable situations you may find yourself in. Your mental attitude is the direct result of what you feel and permit to reside in your mind. If you feed it garbage, it will put out garbage. If you feed it positive thoughts, confidence, happiness, and honesty—it will put out these positive thoughts. Feed your mind daily with positive thoughts that will give you the advantages you desire. Keep your mind on the right things.

The most common litmus test for whether someone is an optimist or a pessimist is whether they see their glass as being half full or half empty. From my viewpoint, either way they both have water, right? That is something to be grateful for.

Commit to seeing the positive in every situation. If you have the habit of being negative, it may even amaze you to realize how negative you really are. Start a gratitude journal and take a few minutes every morning to jot down five things you are grateful for in your life. What you meditate on, you will gravitate toward. Choose your thoughts wisely.

It's been said that breakfast is the most important meal of the day. But nourishing your mind with the right attitude each morning is equally important. How you begin your day controls your day! That may seem easier said than done, especially on busy mornings or during times when you have a lot on your mind. But remember, stress is a part of life. Whatever challenges you are currently experiencing, don't let them keep you from the life—or the happiness—you *want* to experience. As William James once said, "The greatest discovery of my generation is that a human being can alter his life by altering his attitudes of mind." The only place opportunity cannot be found is in a closed-minded person.

Start simple. Think of one thing you can do each morning—even if it's just for five minutes—so you begin the day in the right frame of mind. Ideas include exercise, journaling, or having five minutes to yourself with your favorite cup of coffee.

When you take the time to start the day off right, it really will make a difference—not just to your happiness, but also to your clients, colleagues, friends, and family. And one thing we know for sure is that we all only have a limited number of days here on earth. Each day we can either find something to complain about, or something to be grateful for. It's really up to us.

FAST TIP *3

Commit to Excellence

In his book, *Good to Great*, Jim Collins says, "Greatness is not a function of circumstance. Greatness, it turns out, is largely a matter of conscious choice." Personally, I believe that excellence is to be looked at in the same way. You see, when something is good enough, many may be tempted to leave things as status quo—even when needed improvement is obvious. A person may think there's no need to rock the boat, or they may say to themselves, "It's too much effort to improve."

I want to take this opportunity to challenge you to take on an attitude that when *better* is possible, *good* is not enough. Now is the time to raise the bar for you and for your business if you have not previously had a spirit of excellence in everything that you do. As I tell my children, "If you are going to do something, do your best while you're doing it." You can begin by implementing the tips in this book.

Are you truly committed to excellence? Have you created a business plan? Do you have a written list of professional and personal goals? Are you communicating regularly with your sphere of influence? If you answered "No" to any of these questions, there is no better time than the present to steer your ship in the direction of excellence.

TESTIMONIAL

When my husband and I were looking for a real estate agent to sell our home, we didn't have to think long because we already knew the person we would pick, and that was Michelle Moore. Michelle and I have been friends for many years. Not only are we friends, for which I am grateful, but I have had the privilege of working closely with her for many years by providing administrative support in her real estate business.

Michelle is both extremely knowledgeable about the many facets of the industry, and very hands-on throughout the process of selling and buying a home and other various types of properties. She does her research and is in touch with what the latest marketing techniques are to be able to find the right person to purchase your home as quickly as possible.

She is not only in it for the sale, but she seeks a relationship with you. She has given great care to the referrals we have given her, and we know she will be here and ready to assist us with our future needs as well.

Michelle listens to you and to what your concerns are. I have seen her ability to overcome problems the homeowners have on many occasions, and she always manages to keep a cool head when faced with decisions.

Michelle is a very compassionate and trustworthy person, which is hard to find these days. Another rare quality is giving your best, something my husband and I value. Michelle's display of excellence is evident in everything she does and is reassuring when going through something like selling a home.

–*Tom and Barbara Gibbons*

FAST TIP *4

Develop a Business Plan

"A DREAM WITHOUT A PLAN IS JUST A WISH."
— Bill Cole

Businesses—and people—do not plan to fail; they fail to plan. A business without clear, specific, and time-limited objectives is like a ship without a rudder. It will be cast about at the desire of the winds and currents, with no ability to steer. Without a business plan, how do you:

1. Know the number of listings you need to obtain during any given month?
2. Know the number of buyers you need to represent during any given month?
3. Budget for the amount of money you should invest in marketing for the month?
4. Assess if your conversion rates are where you need them to be?
5. Gauge when to celebrate milestones for your business?
6. Calculate profitability?

When people develop and commit to a clear and compelling vision for the future, with measurable and tangible steps for achievement, they are able to closely monitor how the plan is working at any given moment. Without a plan, how do you know you are succeeding or failing? For instance, to obtain a one-year goal, where would you have to be in nine months? Six months? Three months? By formulating a plan, people become more willing to do what it takes to make the vision a reality. Develop a formal business plan:

1. To prove you are serious about your business.
2. To better understand your competition.
3. To determine your financial needs.
4. To document your marketing plan.

It's shocking to know that most agents don't know their numbers. You are in business for yourself now. That means you are the CEO of your real estate business. CEOs know their numbers. By creating a financial budget, which will include expenses, you will have the information needed to know the number of sales needed in any given day, week, month, or quarter. So, plug in the numbers from your goals.

Over the years, I have always been amazed by the number of agents who treat their businesses like a hobby. They don't set specific hours, they don't plan, and they don't know their numbers. However, they expect business results. This leaves them scratching their heads while wondering why their businesses aren't successful. Taking the time to know how much money you will have, and which areas of your business you are allocating funds to, will lead to knowing if you are going to be profitable at the end of the year.

The next seven tips are designed for assisting you in understanding what components to include when developing your business plan.

FAST TIP *5

Excel in the Power of Brand Positioning

"IF YOU HAVE MORE MONEY THAN BRAINS—
YOU SHOULD FOCUS ON OUTBOUND MARKETING.
IF YOU HAVE MORE BRAINS THAN MONEY, YOU
SHOULD FOCUS ON INBOUND MARKETING."
— Guy Kawasaki

Positioning is one of those nebulous concepts that are kind of hard to pin down—yet at the same time, it is so important to the success of the brand. It is the heart of what the brand is all about, because it encapsulates everything known and understood about the customer, and everything developed for the business.

Positioning is not a buzzword, and it's not marketing "du jour." It is a fundamental aspect of the process of marketing, and honestly, we can't have a business plan without it; therefore, it is imperative to really understand what it is.

Positioning starts with the brand definition but goes much further. In its most simple form, positioning is the mental space that we want to occupy in the mind of the consumer regarding the brand. It's how we want our customers to picture the brand, and it's also the first thing that we want people to think about when they hear the brand name. It's essentially the emotion we want our customers to feel about our brand. It's how we want our brand "positioned" in their minds and it is not logical—it's inherently emotional. If you don't have a brand definition to include in your business plan, take the time to create one now.

FAST TIP *6

Set Goals

"IN ABSENCE OF CLEARLY DEFINED GOALS, WE BECOME
STRANGELY LOYAL TO PERFORMING DAILY ACTS OF TRIVIA."
–Author Unknown

Goal setting is crucial to obtaining success. However, most never do it. Failing to set goals is like setting out on a road trip without a map. Sure you'll end up somewhere, but it probably won't be where you truly wanted to be.

A business can be transformed when you take everything into consideration. Set *realistic* goals and commit them to paper. In Brian Tracy's book, *Goals—How to Get Everything You Want Faster than You Ever Thought Possible*, he claims that "less than 3% of adults have clear written goals with plans on how to achieve them." The key here is *written* goals. Additionally, as I've heard it said many times, you are 80% more likely to reach your goals when they are written. I believe it.

When setting goals for your business:

1. Have short-term and long-term goals.
2. Make your goals specific and measurable with deadlines.
3. Don't set yourself up for failure.
4. Be self-disciplined.
5. Be relevant.

When you wake up each morning with your goals clearly outlined, this gives you purpose and direction every single day. Having direction allows you to incorporate your goals into your daily tasks. Setting your sights on daily goals provides clarity and promotes a more sustained drive.

Know at all times how close you are to achieving your goals by tracking progress with a Monthly Goal Monitoring Worksheet that quickly shows your goals for the month and what you have accomplished at any given time.

If you are going to meet your yearly goal in ten months, congratulations! Consider setting higher goals. Ask yourself if you are close to earning that much-desired sales award, which could be obtained by minimal additional effort on your part. Monitoring your progress ensures that if you are not meeting your goals, you can re-evaluate what is and isn't working in your business. It allows you to adjust the sails and chart a path to better results. Also, always be sure to include continuing education and obtaining designations (See Tip 17) as part of your continued growth, which leads to achieving more goals.

NOTE: When completing a purchase agreement or listing agreement, update the Monthly Goal Monitoring Worksheet at the same time to ensure it is accurate at all times.

BONUS: Visit www.SellingSimplifiedNow.com to receive a FREE copy of *Selling Simplified*'s Monthly Goals Monitoring Worksheet.

A PERSONAL STORY ABOUT GOAL SETTING

I remember my first day at Zaring Homes just like it was yesterday. It was December 1, 1998. The annual awards banquet for the Nashville Division was that day. It took place in a room atop a tall business building with a stunning panoramic view of the entire downtown Nashville area and far beyond.

I was extremely excited to be part of the sales team, was impressed with the company, and believed the quality homes they built were beautiful. I had what I considered to be very big goals and had clearly expressed them during my interview with the VP of Sales and Marketing.

I sat in my seat as various people from different departments walked up to the podium to receive awards. Then they came to the sales department. The Division President announced: "And the Top Sales Performer for the Year is Karen Casada." I was struck by her entire image. She seemed to be the epitome of what one might think a professional real estate agent would look like. She had short hair, perfectly styled, with a conservative black pantsuit. She smiled nicely and as she received her award, I ached to the very core of my being. I wanted to be an award-winning sales professional too and was determined to achieve it!

The beauty of this story is that it not only has a happy ending, it also includes a number of learned valuable lessons. First, I committed my goals to paper, breaking them down by monthly, quarterly, and yearly goal targets (See Tip 6). The quarterly business plan included details of action items and required number of sales (based on average sales price), to get me where I ultimately wanted to be.

I'm happy to report that all my hard work paid off. Not only was I the Top Sales Performer the next year in the Nashville Division, just as Karen had been the previous year, but also on the day of the awards banquet, they announced that I was the Top Sales Performer company-wide (out of six states) for that year!

FAST TIP *7

Create a Marketing Strategy

"THE AIM OF MARKETING IS TO GET CUSTOMERS
TO KNOW, LIKE, AND TRUST YOU."
–Author Unknown

One of the most critical elements of any business plan is your marketing strategy. Most businesses fail because the company, its products, programs, and services provided were never effectively marketed. Ineffective marketing ultimately prevents prospective clients from integrating as customers into your business.

Too often people don't think through that all-important marketing strategy component with the same rigor that they tackle aspects like projected cash flow, short-term, and long-term goals. Or they do put thought and effort into planning for market research, promotion, and positioning—and then never follow through on their great ideas. A solid marketing message is one of the best ways to grab the attention of prospective buyers and sellers. In addition, your marketing message should serve the purpose of communicating to your target market about *why* you are the real estate agent they need to choose.

A frequent issue is that most real estate agents don't have marketing experience. They may be savvy financial advisors or talented in selling—but they're not marketers. Some don't realize that executing a solid marketing strategy is essential to any venture's success; others know it's important but don't know where to begin.

Here's why it's so important: As I say when I teach and coach authors, "You may have the book that could change lives, but it does no one any good if you have five hundred copies of it sitting in your basement because no one knows about it." Marketing is the fundamental building block of any business; it's what drives the business, so it must be a priority.

Here are six points that will have you creating effective marketing messages in no time:

POINT 1 – WHO IS YOUR TARGET MARKET?
An effective marketing message begins by deciding who is your target market. Once you have decided which market you will be speaking to, it is easier to put together a targeted message.

POINT 2 – WHAT IS YOUR MESSAGE?
Your message needs to be more than "My product is great." What problem does your product solve? What is the value you and your service offer? What distinguishes you from your competition?

POINT 3 – HOW CAN YOU HELP YOUR TARGET MARKET?
Now that you have defined the needs of your target market, you must decide the solution that you have to offer them. Clearly present your solution and let your audience know how your solution helps them deal with their current issues.

POINT 4 – PROVE YOUR SOLUTION WORKS.
In this day and age, it isn't enough to tell people you have a solution. By taking this one step further and proving that your solution works helps get your clients on board.

POINT 5 – HOW ARE YOU DIFFERENT?
Being different in today's real estate market is an awesome thing! To
show that your differences will help prospective clients, voice them.

POINT 6 – WHAT IS YOUR BUDGET?
The marketing component of your business plan should include a
budget for money and time. First, determine how much marketing you
can do yourself, if any at all, and how much help you need. You need
a timetable and a professional website that attracts visitors and makes
it easy for them to learn more about you and your service offerings. If
you're handling it yourself, budget for the time it will take to do tasks
like keeping your website active with fresh blog posts once or twice a
week; posting content on social media; and developing pitches to get
print, radio, or television interested. If you plan to pay a professional
for marketing services, use your marketing plan to explore the costs
and timetable, and then budget accordingly.

Whether you're launching a dream or strengthening your existing
business, you need to lay a good foundation with a solid plan. If
marketing isn't an important component of that plan, your rocket to
the moon will likely fizzle and fade.

FAST TIP *8

Develop a Lead Generation Plan

"MARKETING IS A BATTLE OF PERCEPTIONS THAT
IS FOUGHT IN THE MIND OF THE CONSUMER."
— Al Ries and Jack Trout, authors of *The 22 Immutable Laws of Marketing*

If you want to continue to grow your business year after year, you never graduate from generating new leads. Prospecting and marketing are two different ways to generate those new leads. Let's take a look at the differences between the two.

PROSPECTING provides direct contact with potential clients, from which point relationships are established. Most of the activities are inexpensive, but are time and energy intensive.

MARKETING provides indirect contact, which you can use as leverage to develop strong relationships with potential clients. These activities may be expensive, but the long-term rewards far outweigh the up-front costs. Done well, they generate many valuable leads without taking a lot of your time.

Combine the power of high-impact prospecting and marketing to increase your productivity quickly, building upon a positioning package that is attractive to clients.

You may be asking yourself, "What attracts clients?" The answer is easy. It is: content, expertise, resources, your brand, and all that it implies. Ultimately, it all comes down to the perception of value. Value is established by providing great content and expertise and showcasing that with stunning, memorable visuals.

As discussed previously in Tip 7 about creating a marketing strategy, you have to brand yourself (and your business) in a way that connotes value to consumers. Keep in mind that the internet has changed how people purchase products and services. Statistics state, depending on the product, that between 78% and 96% of customers research online prior to buying. These numbers indicate that most potential clients will be researching you online. If they don't like what they find, or if you look like every other agent online, there's no value to the client.

To accomplish "standing out," begin by creating a website with a blog element that showcases your unique business brand. Update your blog so that you can showcase your expertise in real estate on a regular basis. Blogs are easy to maintain and offer loads of flexibility. They're perfect for many business owners, including real estate agents, who want to offer great content, strut their expertise, and bring it all to life in a visual way.

One last thing: stay consistent with keeping your name out there. It's important to remember that during the spring selling season, or whenever you're experiencing a good month, you must continue all regular marketing efforts. When experiencing a great month, it is so tempting to discontinue the marketing. Don't do it! Along with the increased to-do items that come with taking care of buyers and sellers during a busy month, you must maintain those marketing efforts and all other lead generation activities. It's when you stop these important habits that you will experience peaks and valleys that are too common in real estate. Remember, you still have to worry about next month and the month after that, and so on.

TESTIMONIAL

In 2009–2010, my business was in a desperate state, the worst since 1984. The market had shifted and I was busy trying to save a previously very successful career that I had built for over twenty-five years. In efforts to lead generate, I had been working hard trying to capture expired listings and to convert For Sale by Owners. They were ways to connect with anyone needing help with their real estate needs. The rejection was huge and I was so discouraged. Finally, I determined that I needed someone to help me think outside the box.

At that time, we had experienced a change in the Keller Williams Realty market center which I worked. Michelle took over the CEO/ Team Leader position for the office. Upon meeting and spending some one-on-one time with Michelle, I knew she was the one to assist me with fresh ideas to revitalize my business. Upon asking, Michelle eagerly agreed to coach me! I was in the process of working with several buyers purchasing new construction and during a strategy meeting, she suggested a new and unique way for me to lead generate that had never occurred to me. She suggested that I begin cultivating a relationship with on-site agents in the area. She explained that I needed to let them know I was eager to help any of their buyers who had homes to sell before they could purchase a home in the neighborhood they were working. Typically, on-site agents do not list homes outside of their new-home neighborhood.

We began brainstorming creative ways to begin cultivating those relationships. I soon began visiting on-site sales agents. My strategy included dropping by with coffee one week and a light lunch the next. The third week, I'd even drop by with a couple of movie tickets. It was an instant success and resulted in several referrals from those agents!

I am happy to report my business is back on track and thriving. I am now helping many buyers and sellers with their real estate needs. I will be forever thankful to Michelle for agreeing to coach me through one of the toughest times of my real estate career.

—Jane McCracken

FAST TIP *9

Create a Lead Management System

"IT IS NOT YOUR CUSTOMER'S JOB TO REMEMBER YOU. IT IS YOUR OBLIGATION AND RESPONSIBILITY TO MAKE SURE THEY DON'T HAVE THE CHANCE TO FORGET YOU."
— Patricia Fripp

How you manage your incoming leads is crucial to the success of your overall lead generation system. Stop worrying about bringing more leads in if you are not focusing on the harvesting of the leads you already have.

Many real estate professionals make the mistake of taking the lead, making a single phone call, and then tossing it aside. It takes more than that. Cultivating a lead requires time and effort. Whether the consumer is interested in purchasing in one week or in ten months, it still necessitates a system where you remain top of mind. Have a touch plan (explained in the next tip) that systematically communicates and helps to build a relationship with your potential client. What you send out is important. Offer valuable tips and information that will position you as the local real estate expert.

FAST TIP *10

Create a Touch Plan

Over the years, I have been nothing short of horrified by the massive amount of agents (and companies) that fail to have a plan for regularly communicating with the people in their database—if they even have a database, that is. I've seen builders (I'm sure there are hundreds) that have been in business for twenty years or more and do not even have a contact management system. Yes, that means they have zero names, phone numbers, or email addresses. When the market shifted a few years back, one builder had a business that fell to roughly 20% of what it once was, and they were sitting ducks— dead in the water.

You see, having a multi-faceted touch plan is a great way to take control of your business proactively. Someone who is a "sitting duck" has a reactive approach to business, when a proactive approach would be more effective. When the phone rings, they react by answering it. Reactive businesses have no way to maintain consistency and certainly have no way to "drum up" business because they don't have the necessary systems in place to do so.

When covering this topic while coaching and training real estate agents, I always like to point out the obvious—if you are not actively communicating with your sphere of influence, then they are what I like to call "steal-able." Meaning, of course, if they are not hearing from you, then they will forget about you. Forgetting about you offers an environment that makes them "prime for the picking."

While I believe *all* the tips in this book are key components to owning a thriving business, if you choose to only implement a few tips from this book, please be sure this tip is one of them. Begin by proactively creating and implementing a touch program that includes phone calls, direct mail, and emails. Begin by proactively acquiring a system that allows you to automatically email your sphere of influence. Gather any and all names with email addresses that you have, then obtain permission to add them to your database, add them into your system, and begin with a drip email campaign that is clear, concise, and actionable.

FAST TIP ✳11

Manage Your Time

"YOU HAVE TO DECIDE WHAT YOUR HIGHEST PRIORITIES
ARE AND HAVE THE COURAGE—PLEASANTLY,
SMILINGLY, NON-APOLOGETICALLY, TO SAY 'NO'
TO OTHER THINGS. AND THE WAY YOU DO THAT IS
BY HAVING A BIGGER 'YES' BURNING INSIDE. THE
ENEMY OF THE 'BEST' IS OFTEN THE 'GOOD.'"
— Stephen R. Covey

Do you ever feel like there are not enough hours in the day to accomplish all that you need to complete? As a professional who is paid based on performance, there is nothing more important than staying focused on the activities that produce results. Learning that there is a huge difference between being productive versus having a day filled with busyness could be the one breakthrough that you need to take your business to the next level!

The first part of every day should be spent focusing on the most important tasks. Why bother spending hours on time-consuming or low-payoff tasks when you could be focusing on tasks which produce results that actually generate income?

The secret to your future is hidden in your daily routine. You have to be self-disciplined to spend your time wisely. It's all about priorities and the urgency with which you respond to those tasks. By identifying and eliminating unproductive time drains, such as becoming buried in administrative tasks, chasing dead leads, or fretting over unimportant details, you can focus on those activities that bring revenue in the door.

Schedule time into your calendar and then itemize everything you will work on. Once you've done that, number each item and work through your list. Complete what you can during your scheduled time without any interruptions or distractions. Rinse and repeat the next day.

What about those pesky distractions? Between the phone, email, internet, employees, and all other "interruptions," our day can quickly get away from us if we allow it. So turn it all off and choose to stay focused on the task at hand. Do not allow time for a quick vacation on Facebook or an extended stroll down memory lane with an old friend. Cut yourself off from all distractions, work down your list, and reward yourself with a break once complete. You may find that you finish your list much earlier than you anticipate when you are free from distractions, leaving you time to get ahead on tomorrow's tasks or to catch up on your social interactions.

People who choose to live by the "status quo" will always get the results that the masses get. However, if you want superior results, then conduct an audit of your time and the activities that you follow on a day-to-day basis and the results that come from each activity. Don't stay busy just to be busy by filling your time with worthless activities. Figure out what your most productive activities are—and multiply them.

Keep in mind that time is your most valuable resource because it is the only thing that you can't get back. If you lose money, you can gain it back. If you lose time, it is gone forever.

FAST TIP ✳12

Don't Give Up on Tenacity

"LET ME TELL YOU THE SECRET THAT HAS LED ME TO MY
GOAL. MY STRENGTH LIES SOLELY IN MY TENACITY."
— Louis Pasteur

I cannot think of any other profession that's as closely associated
with the term "rejection" as a career in sales can be. I once heard that
rejection is as natural to a salesperson as trail dust is to a chuck-wagon
cook. It simply comes with the territory.

No matter how fantastic your sales skills are, sometimes hearing
"No" will just happen. Instead of internalizing it and letting it
discourage you, realize that you are only that much closer to a "Yes!"
Too many agents give up too soon.

Begin with having the correct frame of mind. Every person getting
into the profession of sales deals with this. It's not about you; it is about
what fits the customer's needs best. Let me repeat that: It is about what
fits the customer's needs best. So there is no need to take it personally if
the prospect doesn't like something you have listed.

Personally, overcoming rejection was something I struggled with
when I first began my real estate career until I found some techniques
that worked for me. First, I would literally tell myself, "I am now
closer to a 'Yes!'" Second, soon I began to realize that one person
was not the end-all be-all to my business that day. By having more

prospects to work with, I automatically watered-down the impact of any single "no sale."

Selling is a game of statistics. Sales professionals get paid by the number of times they close the deal, not by the number of times they strike out. Keep score and know your sales effectiveness numbers so that you can improve your batting average.

Rejection is part of the journey toward success, so don't be insulted or get upset when it happens. In fact, get excited about how you just got closer to your "Yes!" Tenacity is a powerful character trait to develop—and sets you apart from the crowd. As the quote by Wayne Dyer goes, "It's never crowded along the extra mile."

FAST TIP *13

Focus on Helping Others

Look at it like this: You are a real estate professional providing help. Your clients and customers need you. People don't buy or sell a home every day and so are in dire need of help in navigating the process of one of the biggest changes in their lives. And as you assist others in getting what they want and need, your wants and needs will be met and possibly exceeded.

I have always said that I would have been a teacher if only it would have paid more because of the joy it brings me to help and teach others. Instead, teaching, training, and coaching real estate agents throughout the years has been very fulfilling and motivating. It has also reminded me of just how much I know about real estate and the business of selling. I have even gained some insights that I did not expect to acquire while helping others. After all, it is often said that if you want to really learn something—teach it.

Being a real estate professional means doing the right thing for your clients, every time, all the time. Even though real estate professionals have an established set of rules and code of ethics to live by, you should do the right thing because you *want* to—not because you have to. One wise truth of life is that all that is really worth doing is what we do for others. If you haven't done much giving in your life—try it and see how you feel afterwards.

There have been months when I have been so busy helping others that I had no idea just exactly how much money I was earning. Fact is, there are salespeople who look at each buyer or seller and see the amount of money they stand to make from working with that customer or client. This is exactly what *not* to do. If you focus on helping others to get what they want, then what you want—not just what you need to pay your debtors—will come.

FAST TIP *14

Appreciate Enthusiasm

"KNOWLEDGE IS POWER, BUT ENTHUSIASM
PULLS THE SWITCH."
– B.J. Marshall

Enthusiasm is that "certain something" that makes us stand out, pulls us out of the mediocre common places, and turns us into powerful influencers. Enthusiasm is the key that will make other people smile when they are with us. It is the maker of friends, the producer of confidence; and it cries to the world, "I've got what it takes!" It tells everyone that our job is a great job, the company we work for is the best, the goods and services we have are the finest available, and so on, and so on. Clients can sense whether you are passionate about your business or are simply putting in time. If you exude your love for the real estate industry, clients will be eager to connect and embrace with that energy. If you have enthusiasm, you should thank God for it. If you do not have it, then you should get down on your knees and pray for it.

Enthusiasm is contagious. If you catch it, it can help motivate you to sell a home. If your prospects catch it from you, it can motivate them to buy. When you are well prepared, prospecting, listing, showing, and selling homes can be fun. The enjoyment you feel in exercising your talents and knowledge will rub off on your prospects and inspire their confidence in you. Your enthusiasm can provide the sparkle that makes house hunting enjoyable; prospective buyers will choose to work with you rather than with a person who regards the process as a chore. Furthermore, if your clients sense that you are excited about *their* future and you offer a positive experience that fulfills their needs, they will be willing to spread the word about you and the great service you provide—over and over again.

Enthusiastic people radiate energy. They find creative solutions to problems and obstacles and persevere until they make that sale. Enthusiasm provides the impetus to set higher sales goals. And your own enthusiasm attracts more and more prospective buyers, helping you to meet those goals.

Successful people do all the things unsuccessful people don't and won't do. For example, choose to stay enthusiastic when you keep on being rejected. Zig Ziglar once said, "For every sale you miss because you're too enthusiastic, you will miss a hundred because you're not enthusiastic enough." Successful people will go knock on fifty doors and be just as enthusiastic on door number fifty as they were on the very first door.

The last four letters of Enthus*iasm* stand for: "I am sold myself." Through the years, I have had many buyers comment about my level of enthusiasm regarding the homes I showed them. It is because I truly believed in the neighborhood, the builder, the quality of homes, and the designs.

When coaching salespeople, I often teach, "Remember, people will only get as fired up and excited as you are in the process. You set the bar." Truly believe in your daily tasks, opportunities, goals, your company, and your properties. When you get excited about them, there will be no limits to your success.

TESTIMONIAL

Michelle Moore was a joy and a ray of sunshine from the moment we met her. Almost instantly her enthusiasm, professionalism, and passion for her job caught our attention and led us to wanting to have her on our team when building our home.

As an Army Veteran, I would like to think of myself as a people person who has worked with and been around a lot of different folks from all walks of life. Michelle was (and still is) a very trusting, understanding person that you could not help but like. During the five-month process of building a home, I found Michelle to be a very spiritual, Christian person of faith. She was straightforward, honest, and did not lead us on or misguide us in any way. It was clear that she was very professional and knowledgeable in her field. We felt blessed to have Michelle as our real estate agent throughout the whole process and we know she is who we will be calling, when the time comes, with any other real estate needs.

Besides my wife, Army "GSR" friends, my brothers, and very few close friends in my life, Michelle is definitely in my core group of true friends and family.

—Maurice Jenkins

FAST TIP *15

Spend Time with High-minded People

"SURROUND YOURSELF WITH ONLY PEOPLE WHO ARE
GOING TO LIFT YOU HIGHER! LIFE IS ALREADY FILLED
WITH THOSE WHO WANT TO BRING YOU DOWN."
— Oprah Winfrey

People who have accomplished much generally have a different way of thinking and doing. They have drive and a level of commitment that supersedes most. The only difference between you now and you five years from now will be the books you read and the people you spend time with. This means if you spend your time around people who haven't accomplished much, you will be tempted to let the smallness in others bring out the smallness in you.

During my first year in real estate, I remember making friends and going to lunch with the top five agents in my office. The amount of information I learned was amazing. They were active members of the local Chamber, they knew of restaurants coming into the area, they knew the Who's Who of our marketplace, and my goal was always to pick up any crumbs they dropped. They were unconsciously competent and I was constantly amazed at their knowledge. Spending time around those at the top of their "game" showed me how much I really did not know and helped me to realize what I still needed to learn. I was slowly leaving my "conscious incompetence" and taking steps to becoming "consciously competent."

During my second year in real estate, including the beginning of my new-home sales career, I worked with a hugely successful national homebuilder as a Relief Agent. Once again, I made it my business to get to know the top agents who were where I wanted to be. Lunches included listening to terms and discussing various situations that can arise while doing business on-site. The information and lessons learned during those times proved to be invaluable to me as I was well on my way to becoming unconsciously competent. Additionally, life-long relationships were formed during those years and some of those agents are my closest friends today.

If your business is not where you want it to be, take a look around at the other agents in your office. Ask yourself, "Who has a business at the same level that I want to achieve?" Then, ask them out for coffee or lunch. Prepare a list of questions in order to maximize your time together. You are bound to learn many lessons by spending time with people who are where you want to be. Odds are that they are where they are because they have elevated their way of thinking.

If you are brand new to real estate, ask an agent to consider mentoring you. This allows you to learn the ins and outs of the business. Shadow your mentor and learn from his or her experiences. This is an opportune time to ask questions, get advice, seek guidance, and learn what it takes to succeed in the real estate industry. What a golden opportunity to receive "on-the-job" experience!

Spend time with the right people and the right things will come out of you—as long as you remain coachable. Our society is full of people with a mindset of mediocrity, so elevate your thinking to that of a superstar!

FAST TIP *16

Commit to Self-improvement

"WE ARE WHAT WE REPEATEDLY DO. EXCELLENCE
IS NOT AN ACT, IT IS A HABIT."

—Aristotle

Sometimes getting feedback can be an unpleasant experience, especially when it hasn't been requested. But without timely feedback, it's utterly impossible for a person to accurately identify his or her shortcomings, correct bad habits, and profit from mistakes. Coveting sincere feedback and welcoming constructive criticism from customers, associates, and family members could be the difference between where you are today and where you could be tomorrow.

I cannot think of any top-producing sales professionals who have become successful by avoiding critical feedback. Unsuccessful people often reject feedback and avoid taking personal responsibility for their actions. They have difficulty admitting weaknesses and when confronted, they'll frequently respond to feedback by denying responsibility or by lashing out in anger to deflect blame.

Unfortunately, far too many people are "thin skinned" when it comes to receiving feedback and as a result, they often misinterpret sincere criticism as a form of personal attack. It is fairly typical and somewhat understandable for people to become overly defensive and a bit argumentative whenever their personal flaws and shortcomings are held up to the glaring spotlight of criticism. Obviously not all feedback is accurate, sincere, nor given with the purpose of coaching and growth. Nor does every input automatically require action to be taken. However, the key to long-term business success and personal achievement is determined largely not by hard work alone, but by one's ability to glean the kernels of wisdom from the chaff of feedback.

It is important not to put up a wall to avoid feedback, because the same walls that shield you from criticism also block your potential. When is the last time you recall asking your associates or close friends for their honest feedback? Every time I ask, I almost always learn something new about myself that I can build upon.

FAST TIP *17

Commit to Good Education

"NOT ONLY SHOULD YOU BELIEVE IN WHAT YOU ARE DOING,
BUT YOU SHOULD KNOW WHAT YOU ARE DOING."

– Mason Williams

Investing in your education is not only an investment in yourself, but also an investment into your business. Knowledge is the foundation of your business. It is the way to get the skills and experiences you need to stand apart from the crowd in today's competitive marketplace. As real estate agents, we are part of a dynamic, rapidly changing industry, and committing to attending seminars, classes (in person and online), workshops, reading blogs and books, and attending local, state, and national real estate association meetings will only increase your value and credibility to your clients. Set your sights on expanding your real estate knowledge and keeping abreast of the latest trends in your chosen field of real estate.

When considering which classes to take, consider beginning by looking at available designations and focusing your attention in that direction whenever possible. It is a key way that you can ensure your longevity and commitment to excellence while on appointments with prospective clients. You could call it positioning, if you will. Positioning adds credibility to you and your business.

In fact, based on the 2012 National Association of Realtors®

survey data, the median income of Realtors® with at least one designation was $21,100 higher than the median income of Realtors® without any designations.

Although most prospective buyers and sellers are not aware of what the designation abbreviations stand for, there will always be opportunities to explain that those Realtors® who possess them cared enough to spend the time and resources necessary to acquire the highest level of education and skills in the real estate industry.

To learn more about designations, visit:

1. www.realtor.org/designations-and-certifications
2. www.RealtorU.com
3. www.REALTOR.org/education

Please keep in mind that you will not grow by simply learning. You only blossom when you start applying what you have learned. If you do not invest the time and effort to construct a solid foundation for your business, it could seriously take only a huff or a puff to blow your house down.

FAST TIP *18

Use Technology That Increases Efficiency

"THE FIRST RULE OF ANY TECHNOLOGY USED IN A
BUSINESS IS THAT AUTOMATION APPLIED TO AN EFFICIENT
OPERATION WILL MAGNIFY THE EFFICIENCY. THE SECOND
IS THAT AUTOMATION APPLIED TO AN INEFFICIENT
OPERATION WILL MAGNIFY THE INEFFICIENCY."

– Bill Gates

Technology is crucial in today's fast-paced world. There are loads of useful programs, websites, social media platforms, and helpful apps that can be used to streamline your business. However, technology can also swamp us, leaving us mired in a mess of systems, tools, and programs that bog us down, rather than cultivating productivity. Be selective. Incorporate only what works and shut everything else down.

When choosing a system, take the necessary time to research and locate systems that solve real problems. First, they should enable you to disseminate information quickly and easily. Secondly, they should automate daily duties and tasks that you find yourself repeating time and time again. Efficient systems lead to increased profits and contribute to better consumer experiences, which lead to stability and growth for your business.

If you are still avoiding technology, consider the effects Generations X and Y are having on the market. Ranging from ages 18–48, they are 103 million strong, making them a group of consumers and eventual homebuyers that will push the economy forward in the coming years. They readily embrace technology as their preferred communication method. While Baby Boomers prefer face-to-face contact, Generations X and Y are more comfortable with email, voice mail, and text messages, making it *necessary* for today's real estate professional to harness technology to increase awareness and grab the attention of the Generation X and Y homebuyer. If you are not effectively using technology to make your clients' lives easier, you are trailing the industry with regard to effective communication.

FAST TIP *19

Be Open to Change

Change is absolutely necessary in today's fast-paced and demanding environment. Proactive and productive change is something that does not come easy for most people, yet is one of the main reasons successful people succeed. This holds true for companies, too.

If you are not meeting your business goals, ask yourself why. Is it because you are refusing to change where change is most needed? Change isn't always comfortable. But sometimes it is necessary for growth. As the saying goes, "Nothing stops an organization faster than people who believe that the way you worked yesterday is the best way to work tomorrow."

If you are not waking up every morning with a burning desire to do things better—even if it means changing how you run your business—you will end up in a rut. Success involves movement outside of the so-called comfort zone, and will include some risk-taking and experimentation. Take stock of strengths, weaknesses, and opportunities for learning, and honestly evaluate the impact that your actions have on your real estate business.

Don't be afraid to branch out and try something that makes you a little uncomfortable. Stepping outside of your comfort zone can lead you to an amazing place that offers growth potential you never believed possible. The difference between being ordinary and being great lies in your willingness to change.

For example, are you embracing technology or running far away from it? Have you converted to a paperless system with e-signature availability for your clients? Are you excited to learn new things and are you looking for ways to do things better, or are you resisting? Albert Einstein defined insanity as doing the same thing over and over again and expecting different results.

If reading this helps you to realize change has been a challenge for you, make your business a "rut-free" zone right now. Take this opportunity to embrace and welcome change into your life with open arms.

FAST TIP *20

Be Trustworthy

"WE HAVE TO BE ABLE TO COUNT ON EACH OTHER
DOING WHAT WE HAVE AGREED TO DO."
– Phil Crosby

Successful salespeople understand that closing the sale has much more to do with building trust and rapport than it does with issues of lowest price or highest quality. Any engineer will always be quick to tell you that a strong foundation must be laid first before you can build the walls. Likewise, before you can expect your prospect to buy your products or services, he or she must first like and trust you as a person. By the way, if they decide they don't like you, they will also never trust you.

We've all heard betrayal stories: The husband discovers an email between his wife and her boyfriend; the boss catches an employee at lunch with a competitor; the politician lies about, well, everything. From love to business to politics, trust matters. There is no magic formula to building a trusting relationship. However, there are tricks to help you gain trust in a hurry—and keep it.

First, don't skip the "small talk." Far too many salespeople unintentionally sabotage their chances of making a sale by getting right down to business. Second, help your prospect feel comfortable by offering them something to drink—tea, coffee, soda, or water. Many times, just being considerate goes a long way toward earning trust. Third, look for common ground and points of mutual interest such as children's activities, hobbies, sporting events, and of course, the old standby, the weather. Finally, you need to promote yourself as someone whom people trust. Consider giving references that can serve as live testimonials to your abilities and trustworthiness.

Make it a priority to build trust with your clients and your community. Then do absolutely everything possible to maintain that trust. Two real killers to trust are being late to scheduled appointments with your clients, and not doing what you said you were going to do when you said you were going to do it.

A good reputation takes years to build, and only a moment to lose. Walk away from a deal or turn down a client if you have to, in order to maintain your personal integrity. Pay attention to the absence of peace, and follow your gut instinct to sever ties. No deal or amount of money is worth compromising your values and doing irreparable damage to your reputation.

FAST TIP *21

Be Wise

"TALKING COMES BY NATURE, SILENCE BY WISDOM."
– Proverbs

As the saying goes, "Don't un-sell a sold!" As a buyer's agent, it is your responsibility to help your clients find and obtain the best property, at the best possible price, with the least amount of trouble.

It doesn't matter if you have scheduled appointments for a buyer to visit two homes or twenty homes; if they get to a home, fall in love, and want to write up the agreement, call to cancel the rest of the appointments. This is not the time to remind them of the twelve other homes they are scheduled to see that day! Seeing multiple homes can be confusing and complicate matters. If they are placing furniture, you start helping them place the furniture! If they start making a list of things that will be needed, you cheerfully and happily say, "A brand-new home needs brand-new furniture!" Put yourself in their shoes—they are excited to finally find the place they are going to call home.

Years ago, I had set three appointments for new-home communities to show to my clients. The first neighborhood was nice but my clients weren't crazy about any particular floor plan. However, the second neighborhood had the perfect plan built by a national home builder that had a great reputation for outstanding quality. The clients fell in love with a particular floor plan and were ready to pick a home site so they could move forward with an agreement. So, instead of shuffling them off to the third site as planned, I gladly called the agent with the third neighborhood and promptly cancelled the appointment. Those particular clients enjoyed many years in their brand-new home.

Cancelling the appointment was the best thing I could have done for my clients and the next agent on the list, who was waiting at the third property to show it to my clients. Some agents unfortunately lost sight of the primary goal in their pursuit of showing every available property. If your client is ready, willing, and able to sign a purchase agreement, it is your fiduciary responsibility to heed their willingness, and proceed with the paperwork. The last thing you want to occur is that while showing them other properties, the one home they had their eye on gets another offer on it while you were insistent that your clients keep looking.

When faced with this situation, I recommend you do the same thing every time: call to cancel the other showing appointments and pat yourself on the back. Your clients are happy and excited about the home they just found. Mission accomplished!

FAST TIP *22

Dréss for Success

"GOOD CLOTHES OPEN ALL DOORS."

—Thomas Fuller

"You only get one chance to make a first impression." Cliché? Perhaps, but there is truth to this statement. Dressing for success may sound intimidating, expensive, and a bit vain; however, keep in mind that your presentation creates credibility.

According to the Career Center at North Dakota State University, "Whether you like it or not, people size you up in a very short time, actually in only about 2–5 seconds. Your apparel, demeanor, and mannerisms are all factors in influencing what someone else thinks of you and whether you inspire them."

Here are six practical tips to help you make the right impression the first time:

1. WHEN IN DOUBT, CHOOSE TO STAND OUT.

   If you're unsure of what the dress code is—or if there is even a dress code—play it safe by taking the dressier approach. It is always more appropriate and respectable to be overdressed than it is to be underdressed. If nothing else, people will likely compliment you on your jazzed-up look.

2. LESS IS MORE.

You don't need to spend a lot of money on an entirely new wardrobe. Invest in a few classic pieces such as a blazer, a white collared shirt, or a black knee-length skirt, then mix and match a few simple accessories from there.

3. WIN OVER WIVES.

With statistics reflecting that approximately 85% of women make or influence all purchasing decisions, it would be considered good business to be mindful of showing only real estate—nothing more.

4. DRESS TO MATCH THE SITUATION.

When showing new construction or planning to walk farmland, be prepared by having old shoes or rain boots. Consider keeping them in your car for those unexpected appointments that are sure to arise.

5. PASS ON THE PERFUME OR COLOGNE.

Many people have sensitivities or allergic reactions to various scents. Say yes to deodorant but no to strong smells.

6. ORAL HYGIENE COUNTS.

Don't let bad breath be the elephant in the room. Even though you're well groomed and visibly presentable, having bad breath can leave a lasting impression on someone—and not in a good way!

FAST TIP *23

Be Organized

Many good sales people never make it to greatness because of one reason—they're disorganized. They spend valuable time (which equals missed opportunities and money) constantly looking for something. If it isn't one thing, it's another. Typically, they don't have a system at all or they have a system that's way too complicated to work effectively and efficiently. Keep systems simple.

Throughout the years, I have seen agents try to color-code and alphabetize their files by distinguishing by one criteria versus another. By the time I finished hearing about the newly created system, I was exhausted just thinking about how it was bound to fail, prior to it even being implemented. The trouble with getting organized, if you are not careful, is that pretty soon you will pay more attention to the organization than to what you're getting organized for.

Start by finding or creating a good system that works and is quick, easy, and simple for you—and stick with it. A system that meets these requirements will also allow any team member to find what they are looking for, at any given time, on any client. A system like this works no matter the volume of the database.

Wondering about my system? My system was created nearly twenty years ago and has had no changes since its inception. It meets all requirements listed in the above paragraphs. Additionally, this system has worked flawlessly for my five-million-dollar-producing years, as well as my nearly twenty-two-million-dollar-producing years. The shopping list is short. It will require the purchase of a few black sharpie markers and a ⅓ cut center tab only (letter size) manila file folders, both of which can be found at your local business supply retailer. Once purchased, you will have all you need to organize client files. No fancy colored markers needed, no varied tab positions allowed, and no expensive label maker required. And no, you don't have to use the latest smartphone app to be successful, either!

FAST TIP *24

Be Creative

"AN ESSENTIAL ASPECT OF CREATIVITY
IS NOT BEING AFRAID TO FAIL."
– Edwin Land

In general, being successful takes creativity. Whether you are writing descriptions to explain the look and feel of a newly listed home, or overcoming prospective home buyers' objections, or problem solving a delay in a closing, being creative is required on a daily basis. The truth is, problems are actually the basis of all creativity. They are like the soil into which new possibilities can flourish. We would not be challenged to be creative if we did not have a problem to solve in the first place.

Like I said earlier—the only place opportunity cannot be found is in a close-minded person. So, have an open mind and dare to think outside of the box. Work hard to find creative solutions to problems and obstacles, and persevere until you make that sale.

Generally speaking, one of the most effective ways to approach any problem is to ask questions about it. The greatest thing about questions is that your brain automatically starts working on them as soon as you ask them. Not only that, but your brain will continue working on them in the background, even when you're not aware of the process.

Here are five questions to ask yourself when a problem arises and you want to creatively find a solution:

1. WHAT PROBLEM ARE YOU FACING?

This question helps you to establish your current issue. Many times you cannot fix a problem because you don't even know what the problem is. It also focuses your attention on the state of mind that is feeding the problem. For example, you might conclude, "I am overwhelmed by my priorities."

2. WHAT IS YOUR IDEAL OUTCOME?

As Albert Einstein once said, "You cannot solve a problem with the same mindset that created it." Your ideal outcome would, therefore, be a mindset that allows you to solve the problem. For example, you may decide, "My ideal outcome is to be confident about how to deal with my priorities."

3. WHAT'S GOOD ABOUT DEALING WITH THIS PROBLEM RIGHT NOW?

Chances are you may be looking at this issue as "the glass is half empty." All situations have their pros and cons. This question can help you see the glass as half full. Look at what you answered to Question #1 and see if you can find any benefits from working through this issue. It might be helping you to build skills, activate your creativity, or allow something else to occur that might otherwise not happen.

4. WHAT NEEDS TO BURN AWAY SO THAT THE RIGHT SOLUTION CAN MANIFEST?

Naturally occurring forest fires happen to keep our ecosystem in balance. The canopy of old-growth trees can completely block sunshine from reaching the forest floor where important plant life requires the sun to flourish, in order to feed the rest of our ecosystem. Metaphors like this help to open up the creative mind. What needs to burn away in your thought processes in terms of an assumption, a mindset, or point of view that may be blocking you from getting back in the flow with this situation?

5. IF YOU WERE EXCEPTIONAL (AT THE TASK REQUIRED),
WHAT WOULD YOU DO THAT YOU ARE NOT DOING NOW?
This question helps you think outside of a limited view you may have of your abilities. Imagine you are someone who could easily sort this situation out. For example, you may ask yourself, "If I were exceptional at confidently dealing with my priorities (instead of being overwhelmed by them), what steps should I be taking that I'm currently not?"

FAST TIP *25

Know Your Market

Professionals never guess—they make it their business to know their business. This includes knowing the market and knowing how to price real estate appropriately. They take the time to view comparable homes and other real estate for sale, in order to help their clients establish an accurate and competitive price.

Gathering and understanding positive and negative information on real estate markets takes time and effort. You'll need to do your homework. Study local pricing. Know the area and its values. Your clients want to work with someone who knows the business and the area completely. With tools like the Multiple Listing Service (MLS), you can find accurate market comparables, days on market (DOM), tax information, and much more.

FAST TIP *26

Price It Right

"PRICE IS WHAT YOU PAY. VALUE IS WHAT YOU GET."
—Warren Buffet

Sounds simple, right? However, pricing a property is not so simple.
In fact, it is much more complicated than it sounds. There are three
components of a home's worth: Price, Value, and Cost.

- PRICE: When deciding if a property is priced correctly, price
  is what the home should be worth today. Unfortunately, sellers
  sometimes don't price their homes accurately, so what you really
  want to look at is fair market value. This is what the seller should
  reasonably be asking for their property. Recently sold properties
  are used to help determine fair market value. These sales should
  be recent, preferably within the last six months, and should be
  similar in size and upkeep to the property a buyer is considering.
  However, keep in mind that this Comparative Market Analysis,
  or CMA, may not include all the details. The current condition,
  location, and surroundings, as well as the view from the
  property, can all affect the price of a house. A Realtor® should
  be certain to include details like these in the CMA. Appraisals
  can also help figure out a home's fair market value, but there is
  no exact science in pricing.

- VALUE: The value of a property is established by the prospective buyer. Value is an opinion of what the prospective buyer thinks the home is worth, based on how they're going to use it. Value could be calculated based on a person's lifestyle, so it may be different for everyone. For example, a home near a golf course could be less valuable for someone who does not play golf than it would be for someone who does.

- COST: Sellers believe a home is worth what they paid for it, plus how much was spent on improvements and other costs. In reality, when a seller improves a home, the value of the property is increased, not the cost. Since value is based on the buyer's preferences, improvements and other extras are all subjective. A seller could receive dissimilar offers from potential buyers because they have made personal conclusions about the home's value.

Buyers and sellers need to remember that the Comparative Market Analysis is just a starting point, and that value and cost are both subjective. All of these details should be discussed with your sellers, and every property needs to be closely inspected to make sure it aligns with a prospective buyer's needs and budget.

Additionally, the three top priorities for sellers when they first list a property on the market are price, price, and condition. Yes, price is the number one priority and the number two priority—it is that important. If a seller wants to sell quickly, minimize hassles, and get the highest sales price possible—pricing it right rules the roost every time.

FAST TIP *27

Keep Perspective on the Market

"WE CAN COMPLAIN BECAUSE ROSE BUSHES HAVE THORNS,
OR REJOICE BECAUSE THORN BUSHES HAVE ROSES."
—Abraham Lincoln

Much of the media would like you to believe that the real estate market is national. However, much like the weather, it is not national. This means that even when the Las Vegas, Texas, and California markets are in a slump, it does not mean that you cannot be experiencing your best year ever. Let's say your city's real estate market is experiencing a decline, but you just picked up a "ready, willing, and able" buyer today—an "A" prospect. How's your business? By all accounts, your business is doing pretty good.

When considering perspective, and its important role in a successful real estate career, I liken it to that glass with water we are always hearing about. Some like to see the glass half full while others like to see it half empty. If your immediate response is seeing the glass as half empty, I suggest you change your perspective. See the positive in the situation. Celebrate the 50% that is there, not the 50% that is not there.

Now make no mistake, I am not talking about being delusional here. It is important to stay in touch with reality and know the cold, hard facts regarding the true status of your business. However, you can only eat an elephant one bite at a time. With each bite, celebrate the accomplishment. See the accomplishment for what it is—a positive step in the direction you want to go for your business. It is another step toward reaching the goals that you have set for yourself and your business. Use small celebrations and acknowledgements as a way to encourage yourself and remain motivated—two things we all could use more of at times.

Taking perspective a step further, you need to arm yourself with the information needed to speak informatively about current market conditions. For example, keep up with the local Realtors® Board in your area. Most Boards send out statistics on a monthly basis and show comparisons from the previous year. As your current clients and potential clients ask you about the state of the real estate market, because they will, it will behoove you to know the local numbers. There is no better way to diffuse misperceptions about current market conditions, and to even build credibility as a professional, than to educate current and potential clients by sharing factual, third-party information, as well as to continue to explain how the real estate business is local—not national.

FAST TIP *28

Take the Responsibility Seriously

Remember the importance of what you do. It matters. To your client, a home is more than just a roof over his or her head. Sometimes agents tend to forget this is a big investment, if not the biggest, for the homebuyer, and it isn't *just* another transaction. This is the place the clients will call home. The place they may raise their children. Home is the place people come to relax every night after a hard day at work. "Home Sweet Home" is more than a place to hang your hat; more than four walls and a roof. Home is where the heart is. It is an investment, an expense, a retreat, a responsibility, a personal expression, and much, much more.

Through the years, I have been asked many times about my success in real estate and about what I attribute my success to. The answer has always included my ability to remember how important it is to help people buy or sell the place they call home. I know this sounds super simple, however, I have heard many agents speak in ways that clearly indicate they have lost sight of that important detail. Simply put, it's a big deal.

When you deal with large amounts of money every day, like agents do, it can become easy, over time, to forget that you are dealing with people's emotions and dreams. If ever you find yourself thinking your clients are being overly picky or start wondering to yourself, "Why are my clients fretting over every little thing?" stop and put things in perspective by reminding yourself that this is one of the biggest, if not *the* biggest, investment these clients will ever make. Then, feel honored to be the agent they chose to help them navigate through this process.

TESTIMONIAL

My wife and I had been thinking about looking for a new home for several years and had instructed our friend Michelle to keep an eye out for homes that we might like. Very soon, Michelle set up a time to show us several homes she believed would be a great fit for us. Michelle sensed my anxiety and calmed my fears from the moment we were in the car heading toward our first destination. I didn't even know what I didn't know, which was unnerving, but she assured me that *she* did know and was the reason I wasn't doing this alone.

As I entered the foyer of the first home we visited, something seemed different. The floors were hardwood, but they were four inches wide. I'm strange in that I typically don't like hardwood, but this was unique and I liked it. Then we walked into the living room, which had four huge windows out to the back of the house. Bam! It hit me like a ton of bricks. You could see for miles—twelve miles to be exact. The house was on the downward slope of a hill that leveled off onto the 15th fairway of a golf course. I play golf. I staggered through the living room into a huge, inviting kitchen, pausing only briefly to notice that it, too, was perfect.

I had to go out onto the back deck. It was fourteen feet up, but with the terrain quickly sloping downward away from you, it gave you the feeling of being much higher than you really were, and you could see over the next two hills. "This! I want *this*! *This* is what *I* want!" I shouted, quoting one of my favorite Steve Martin characters from the movie *Dirty Rotten Scoundrels*. I could see Michelle smile knowingly. She knew what she was doing bringing me here.

As she showed me and my wife around the rest of the house, I realized it fit us like a glove. And though we visited several homes, we ended up buying the first one we saw. Michelle's understanding of our wants, needs, and concerns translated to a nearly stress-free experience.

Her warm professionalism led to complete trust. She never lost track of the fact that this was a big deal to us, no matter the price point. And for that, we're grateful.

–John and Christy Kirchner

FAST TIP *29

Learn the Three Modes of Communication

"THE MOST IMPORTANT THING IN COMMUNICATION
IS TO HEAR WHAT ISN'T BEING SAID."
– Peter Drucker

There are three modes of communication operating simultaneously as you speak with other people: your words, the tone of your voice, and your body language. Your prospect's subconscious mind is processing all of these signals at once. How they process these cues from you impacts whether the prospect likes, trusts, and ultimately purchases from you.

WORDS

Cultivate the use of your most valuable selling tool—the spoken word. Words can be weak or powerful. There are two types of words you will want to use in real estate:

1. EMOTIONAL WORDS AND PHRASES

   Adopt the practice of using emotional words (sometimes also referred to as "build the dream" words, or picture-painting words).

Powerful words are emotional words that target the emotions, rather than the brain. They excite, stimulate, and cause the blood to warm up. They prepare the listener for action! Well-rehearsed key phrases are instrumental and enhance your sales presentation. Some popular examples are: "convenient," "decorative," "impressive," "spacious," "treed," and "beautiful."

2. POSITIVE WORDS AND PHRASES

Adopt the use of positive words because they build *value*. Another way to put it is that although you cannot change the price, you can change the value of the home simply by changing some of your vocabulary. Some examples are: home "site" instead of "lot"; "custom" features instead of "standard" features; and "initial investment" instead of "down payment."

TONE OF VOICE

As professional communicators, we have the choice of which words and phrases we accentuate for added emphasis and meaning. By slowing down, speaking softly, and emphasizing key words that we want to stand out, we can maximize the effectiveness of our spoken communication.

BODY LANGUAGE

Research has shown that expert communicators are sensitive to their customers' body language and that these unspoken indicators—"non-verbals"—can speak volumes about the customers' readiness to make a buying decision. Make it a priority to recognize these non-verbal signals, and learn to adjust your presentation accordingly.

FAST TIP *30

Learn Temperament Styles

"WHEN PEOPLE SEE YOUR PERSONALITY
COME OUT, THEY FEEL SO GOOD, LIKE THEY
ACTUALLY KNOW WHO YOU ARE."
—Usain Bolt

Do you ever wonder why you seem to have a natural connection with some customers, while with others the effort produces a separation more like oil and water? That's because we respond intuitively to the natural chemistry (or lack thereof) that exists between temperament styles. Our temperament style not only determines our behavioral traits, body language patterns, and buying style, but it also influences our compatibility with other people.

While there are certainly many factors that steer the direction of the selling process, by far the most important factor is your ability to relate to your prospect's temperament style. Once you learn how to quickly and accurately determine your prospect's temperament style, you are armed with the knowledge of how to communicate their way. (More on this with the next tip, the Platinum Rule.) By doing this, you have the ability to help people like you better, trust you more, assist in making the sales process flow more smoothly, and close more sales in less time.

Also, keep in mind that each of these temperament styles tends to define "superior customer service" from a slightly different point of view. Upon identifying each of the styles, you will be able to truly customize your service to fit your customers' expectations.

There are four main personality styles and all individuals possess all four, but what differs from one to another is the extent of each. For most, these types are seen in shades of gray rather than black or white, and within that, there is an interplay of behaviors, otherwise known as blends. The determination of such blends starts with the primary (or stronger) type, followed by the secondary (or lesser) type.

Research in the field of psychology tells us that we are born into one of four primary temperament styles (Aggressive, Expressive, Passive, or Analytical). A person's temperament style is determined genetically. Each of these types has its own unique contribution.

AGGRESSIVE

Strength: Very active in dealing with problems and challenges.

Weakness: Very quick to make decisions—sometimes without all pertinent information.

EXPRESSIVE

Strength: Tends to be emotional, convincing, enthusiastic, and optimistic.

Weakness: Tends to ignore data and facts, and relies too heavily on feelings.

PASSIVE

Strength: Desires to please others, needs security, and does not like sudden change.

Weakness: Tends to be so agreeable that it is hard to discern their true thoughts.

ANALYTICAL

Strength: Thrives on any detailed information available, and easily grasps financing concepts.

Weakness: Difficulty with finalizing decision and dislikes vagueness of any kind.

FAST TIP *3₁

Forget the Golden Rule—Go Platinum

"IT TAKES MANY GOOD DEEDS TO BUILD A GOOD
REPUTATION, AND ONLY ONE BAD ONE TO LOSE IT."
— Benjamin Franklin

Years ago, I was attending a class that was one in a series of classes required to earn the Graduate, Realtor® Institute (GRI) designation. At one point, the instructor made a statement that I will never forget. He said, "If you will just return your clients' calls and do what you say you are going to do when you say you are going to do it, you will be in the top 2% of Realtors® in the real estate business." After gasping and looking around the packed classroom, I saw something even more shocking. No one else seemed surprised by the instructor's comment. Everyone else in the room (except naïve me) already knew that a large number of agents don't return their clients' calls and emails, and don't do what they commit to do when they say that they will do it.

Through the years, I have heard many people talk about how they live by the Golden Rule: "Treat people like you'd like to be treated." And that is good. However, I challenge you to live by the Platinum Rule. It simply states, "Treat people like *they'd* like to be treated." Apply this principle at all times—whether personally or professionally related—and see how all areas of your life will be transformed.

For example, while selling on-site for a large national home builder, I would ask customers which way they preferred to be communicated with regarding the purchase of their brand-new home. I would mark their registration card and file, reminding myself how best to communicate with them, whether by calling, texting, or emailing. I found that by implementing this detail into my systems, my productivity increased. I spent less time calling all their numbers only to leave voicemail messages.

I have been amazed at the number of people who prefer to text since I like to actually speak with my clients. By implementing the Platinum Rule, I focus on how the customer wants to be treated and I am able to provide a higher level customer experience for clients.

FAST TIP *3₂

Listen, Listen, and Listen Some More

"A GOOD LISTENER IS NOT ONLY POPULAR EVERYWHERE,
BUT AFTER A WHILE HE KNOWS SOMETHING."
—Wilson Mizner

The #1 complaint people have had about an agent they hired or considered hiring is that they felt the agent did not listen to them. Surprisingly enough, superior customer service is linked more with your ability to actively listen than it is with imparting your knowledge and expertise.

One of the most valuable ways you can show honor to your clients is by listening to them. Not only does that demonstrate that they are important to you—if you're listening well, they are much more likely to give you helpful clues that will enable you to provide the best service for them. Ask open-ended questions and listen to the answers. These answers can provide clues that reveal hidden expectations and insight to what their buying or selling triggers really are.

For example, showing buyers a three-bedroom home when they have repeatedly shared that they need four bedrooms will frustrate the buyers and lead them to feel that you do not listen to them. The proof is in the pudding here—by showing them three-bedroom homes, you didn't listen.

Another important piece of information to remember is that every sale has five basic obstacles to overcome: no need, no money, no hurry, no desire, and no trust. This last one is easily eliminated by listening.

Additionally, by listening attentively, we are able to reflect back on our customers' needs throughout the entire sales process. This causes your customers to see that you are listening and that you care about their needs, which will, in turn, cause your customers to be loyal because they feel your sincerity. Make the effort to really hear them loud and clear.

THE ART OF LISTENING

A salesman at a sporting goods store gave a customer who had inquired about a new outboard motor a big smile and went into a long story expounding upon the virtues of the particular motor he wanted to sell. The salesman talked at length about several features of the motor in which the customer was not particularly interested, and inadvertently emphasized things the man did not want in a motor. The salesman talked and talked and talked. The customer listened as well as he could, but the longer the salesman talked, the more the customer resented him. Even though he wanted a motor, he finally left without one.

A couple of days later, the man walked into another sporting goods store. A salesman approached him and asked what he would like to see. Learning that the customer was interested in an outboard motor, he asked if it would be used on a lake or on another body of water, and if it was for fishing or high-speed pleasure riding. As the man related the uses he had in mind, the salesman listened carefully and asked questions. Then, he showed a motor that best suited the customer's needs. The man purchased the motor.

The lesson to be learned here is that God gave us two ears and one mouth, and that listening is usually better than talking. It will result in more sales and more customers.

FAST TIP *33

K.I.S.S. (Keep It Simple and Straightforward)

"LIFE IS REALLY SIMPLE, BUT WE INSIST
ON MAKING IT COMPLICATED."
— Confucius

Sellers want to sell and buyers want to buy. However, this is not something they do every day. You are needed to lead the way. In fact, buyers and sellers are expecting you to take the lead. In general, buyers do not know how to buy and sellers do not know how to sell.

While under a tremendous amount of stress, buyers are busy navigating the overwhelming process of purchasing a home, and sellers are busy navigating the overwhelming process of selling a home. In fact, statistics show that buying and selling a home are two of the five most stressful times in a person's life. They need you to assure them that you will be there to guide them through the entire process.

There are a couple of things you can do to help buyers and sellers sail through the process. First, use simple terminology when referring to real estate "lingo." Second, avoid using confusing acronyms that they will not be familiar with. By keeping everything simple and easy to understand, you are minimizing misunderstandings and stress, which fosters a pleasant experience for all those involved—including you.

FAST TIP *34

Grade Prospect Quality

In many ways, grading prospect quality goes back to Tip 11, which covers the seriousness of managing your time effectively. As a professional who is paid based on performance, there is nothing more important than staying focused on the activities that will produce results. With that in mind, it only makes sense to incorporate that principle into deciding which prospective clients to spend time with by grading the quality of each and every prospect.

Whether you categorize your clients with A, B, and C; 1, 2, and 3; or cold, warm, and hot; it really doesn't matter as long as you prioritize them and spend your time with the ones most likely to be converted to an actual listing or purchase.

The traffic quality scale is defined as:

A TRAFFIC   Persons who are ready, willing, and able to purchase a home.

B TRAFFIC   Persons who are willing but either not yet ready or not yet able to do so, because they have a home not yet sold, although it is on the market.

C TRAFFIC   Persons who are not financially qualified or not currently motivated to buy.

Consider instituting a new policy that your buying clients are qualified by a preferred mortgage professional prior to your showing them a home. Your time is valuable and with the rising cost of fuel, driving around touring homes your buyers may or may not even qualify for is not the way to stay within your business budget, nor is it a good use of your time or theirs. You are not a tour guide. You are a real estate professional. Please remember that the time you are investing into a "B" or "C" prospect is also time that you cannot be lead generating for "A" prospects. Ask yourself, "What business am I willing to give up while working with these people who are not ready and/or able to buy right now?"

Plus, if you show several $200,000 homes and they only qualify for a $175,000 home, the buyer will now have an even harder time finding a home in their budget, since they have gotten used to looking at all those more expensive homes.

I heard a saying a long time ago that says, "You teach people how to treat you." Begin taking charge of leading your buying clients through a simple process of purchasing a new home. Do not allow them to complicate the matter by potentially wasting their (and your) time by looking too early.

FAST TIP *35

Provide Added-value Services

"YOU CAN START RIGHT WHERE YOU STAND AND
APPLY THE HABIT OF GOING THE EXTRA MILE BY
RENDERING MORE SERVICE AND BETTER SERVICE
THAN YOU ARE NOW BEING PAID FOR."
— Napoleon Hill

We have all had at least one of those buyers who refused to get out of the car, due to absolute disdain for a home and its appearance from the driveway. It never ceases to amaze me how a home with no curb appeal can ruin the chance of even getting a look inside—you'll go from sixty to zero in no time flat.

This subject reminds me of a book by Malcolm Gladwell, *Blink: The Power of Thinking Without Thinking.* This is a book about rapid cognition, explaining the kind of thinking that happens in the blink of an eye. When you meet someone for the first time, or in this case, drive up and see the façade of an available home for the first time, your mind takes about two seconds to jump to a series of conclusions—the first impression, if you will. *Blink* is a book about those two seconds, because those instant conclusions that we reach are powerful and important. Builders spend thousands of dollars on putting their best foot forward for that first impression of all who visit their communities. Notice that I did not say, "For all those who cross the threshold of the model home." Savvy builders understand that the first impression begins when a prospect enters into the neighborhood.

Now, this is where I'd like to challenge you to take your business to the next level. By offering professional advice and sharing detailed knowledge on related areas of the real estate business, you have the ability to shed light where light needs to be shed—whether your client realizes it or not. I refer to this as an added-value service.

This is when you can offer design tips and trends, share staging knowledge, and advise builders and buyers on vital floor-plan features prior to beginning construction, and much more. For example, at a listing appointment, you prepare a to-do list of repairs for the sellers to complete prior to your listing of the home—nothing unusual. That list includes painting a currently pink bedroom to a neutral color. The added-value service is when you pull out your Sherwin-Williams paint deck and show them which colors you recommend and choose one while sitting together. This gets the sellers out of the overwhelming chore of choosing a color, which is something they typically know nothing about, and ensures that you don't show up to list the home a few weeks later to see that they painted the room a white color that includes a peach or green undertone.

This subject isn't about becoming a decorator, painter, or a landscape architect. This topic is about providing guidance by knowing the basics that help you ultimately serve your clients to the best level possible. Begin by taking staging classes, reading articles on all things related to paint, obtain a paint deck of current colors, and learning about tips and tricks for landscaping and flooring. Take it from me, when you provide added-value services you will watch your business grow by leaps and bounds.

TESTIMONIAL

I cannot express what a big help Michelle was when it came to selling our home. She went above and beyond in answering all of our questions, most of them repeatedly, and making sure we really understood the process. No detail was too big or too small.

We had an unexpected situation with our home, which was frustrating to us, but she remained calm. She kept assuring us that everything would be fine and repeatedly said, "Do not worry. I will be the first one to tell you if you need to worry."

She even made calls that were outside of her responsibilities to get our home sold. And she remained helpful long after her job was completed.

I cannot express how impressed my husband and I were throughout the entire process of working with her. We've worked with Realtors® who were good, as well as those who were really bad, but Michelle is by far the best!

—*Sanford and Karen Robinson*

FAST TIP *36

Know the Details

"THE DIFFERENCE BETWEEN SOMETHING GOOD AND
SOMETHING GREAT IS ATTENTION TO DETAIL."
– Charles R. Swindoll

For years, I have said, taught, and coached sales professionals that "The deal is in the details." Really, no detail is too small or too trivial. For the most part, if they are asking about the detail, it is important. Buyers are unable to move forward with the buying decision if they are not armed with the necessary information needed, in order to make an informed decision.

Years ago, I worked in a very popular, professionally decorated model home that featured the owner's retreat on the main level. The home included a customizable feature, at an investment of $9,900, to add a private sitting room with beautiful round columns on half walls and added a total of 42 square feet of space to the owner's retreat closet space—a measurement that I figured with my scale and official blueprints. It turned out to be a profitable four minutes to figure out that square footage.

Prospects would tour the home, love the plan, and laugh as I explained the details—down to the 42 square feet of additional closet space. Talk about building credibility! That extra closet space was the most expensive custom feature available for that floor plan. However, after hearing all the details, it seemed quite the bargain. It may have been the most expensive item, but it was also the most frequently chosen item.

Examples of Details That Buyers Need to Know:

1. Is the microwave vented directly to the outside?
2. What type of fireplace—wood burning, direct vent, or ventless?
3. How high are the ceilings in every part of the home?
4. Is there any floored attic space? If so, is it engineered to be load-bearing for storing items?
5. Are fences allowed? What types? From which point of the home does the fence originate?
6. Are there home owner's association fees and are they paid monthly, quarterly, or annually?
7. If there is a swimming pool, is it Olympic-sized? Is there a neighborhood swim team?
8. Is there a lifeguard?
9. What are the dates that the pool is open?
10. If there are sidewalks throughout the community, where are they located?
11. Where are the light posts and electrical boxes going to be located?

FAST TIP *37

Provide Information

Throughout my career, I have often said that it is my job to make sure that my clients make an intelligent decision. Facts and statistics arm people with what it takes to make an informed decision. Like the familiar old saying goes: "Confused minds say no."

In an industry where the average prospect doesn't purchase or sell a home very often, creating a memorable experience is a must. Producing a "wow" experience will leave a lasting impression that your client will remember whether they purchase in three years or ten.

Of course, not all transactions are created equal, but there are specific needs that most homebuyers share. As a professional, it is more imperative than ever to impart your expertise, wisdom, and compassion while guiding clients through the process.

Regardless of whether they are purchasing for the first time or have purchased multiple homes in the past, buying a home is one of the most stressful events in a person's lifetime that can be positively impacted by the professional nature of the agent.

FAST TIP *38

Learn the
Sales Process

"EXPERTS HAVE THEIR KNOWLEDGE IN ORDER."
— Nido Qubein

If you have a real estate business, you are a salesperson. However, surprisingly, many real estate agents don't know how to sell. And I suspect many agents do not even see themselves as sales professionals.

Using a process gives you control of the situation because you know at all times where you are going—with your clients coming along. Buyers don't want to be sold, they want to buy. Taking control is something we do in our customer's best interest. The process is about leadership and about taking people to places that they cannot get to on their own, while they are still feeling comfortably in control of a buying decision.

While the sales process can seem overwhelming at times, it truly is about mastering the basics of the sales process. There's no need to overcomplicate matters.

Here are the five steps in the sales process:

1. MEET AND GREET
   Establish rapport and obtain names, phone numbers, email addresses, mailing addresses, prices, urgency, preferences, and anything else that could be useful throughout the sales process.

2. QUALIFY

Determine the buyers' needs by asking open-ended questions to determine commitment, opportunity, motivation, money, and action (C.O.M.M.A.).

3. DEMONSTRATE

Match the clients' needs to properties that meet their criteria, then show the properties and discuss community and area information. Remember to have a planned presentation.

4. CLOSE

Summarize, handle final objections, ask for the sale, and complete the purchase agreement.

5. FOLLOW UP AND/OR FOLLOW THROUGH

During the time period between signing a contract and closing on the property, it is imperative that a professional real estate agent continue with a follow-through plan. This plan is two-fold. You can solicit referrals all the while dealing with the possibility of "Buyer's Remorse." Continue this plan for at least thirty days after the closing of the property. This step directly impacts the amount of referrals you will receive and cannot be overlooked. If a purchase agreement has not been completed, proceed with a strategic follow-up plan.

If the property is new construction, a stage would be inserted after the #3 Stage: Demonstrate. The added step is Site/Select. This step includes showing the actual home site that would be available to build the floor plan of their choice, or to visit available opportunities that are under construction or recently completed.

It is imperative that you thoroughly cover each step in the sales process. Never, ever omit a step. Doing so will most certainly lead to paying dearly later in the sales process.

FAST TIP *39

Have a Planned Presentation

Always having a planned, not canned, presentation prepares you for any surprises in the sales process. This leads me to a saying I heard years ago: "Proper planning prevents poor performance." And in sales, this is no different.

An example of this preparation would be having a detailed, full-color listing presentation that covers each temperament style's wants and needs. Be sure to cover hot topics that sellers not only want and always ask about (like how and where you are going to market their home), but also include other topics that sellers *should* be asking about and just don't know to ask. For example, consider including recent statistical numbers from the National Association of Realtors®, detailing the number of buyers that begin their new-home search online.

Throughout the years, I have been amazed at the number of agents I have coached or taught that had a few pieces of paper slapped together that they considered as their listing presentation. Or worse, there may be no presentation at all! This is not the time to "wing it." We are talking business here—big business! Ultimately, a listing presentation should compel the sellers to have no doubts about hiring you once the meeting is over.

While on this topic, I would like to share that every listing appointment I have ever been on has always resulted in my ability to obtain the listing—including builders. I share this not to brag or boast; rather to ensure that I fully communicate the importance of planning and perfecting that plan, which always leads to success. The road to my success is found in covering important areas thoroughly, while keeping the process simple and easy to understand.

Other times that call for a planned presentation would include when meeting with buyers to sign a buyer's representation agreement, and when showing properties—a home or land. Always have a presentation that strategically includes such details as asking questions that require the prospect's active participation, and how to build value by using features and benefits.

TESTIMONIAL

With the birth of our daughter in 2009, we officially outgrew the 900-square-foot home I purchased as a bachelor in 2001. The housing market was sluggish, and we knew that selling our home would require the right Realtor®. So we decided to interview real estate agents to get a better understanding of what we needed and what they could offer.

The first agent we interviewed tried to convince us more about the worthiness of her company than the plan she had for selling our house. She also had a difficult time answering any questions that were not in her company's notebook. Overall, her plan seemed underwhelming and impersonal.

The second Realtor® we interviewed was Michelle Moore. We were referred by friends who had recently sold their home with her. Within moments of meeting her, we knew she was personable, passionate, and prepared. She listened to us, counseled us, shared her experiences, and laid out a plan to get our place sold. As she went over her multi-faceted marketing plan for our home, I thought to myself, "Wow, she really thought of every aspect, and on such a personal level." As teachers, my wife and I appreciated the time Michelle took to educate us on the whole home-selling process. When she left our home that day, we knew she was the right Realtor® for us. My wife said with both fear and excitement, "We better start packing because she is going to sell this house out from under us." And that's exactly what she did! Our house sold and closed within four short months.

We had trusted Michelle to help us sell our old home, and we trusted her when she led us to our new home. Trust is as important as knowledge, experience, and drive. If we had not trusted her, we could have ended up frustrated and hopeless with someone else. We are so thankful for someone who presented the total package.

—Ted and Shanna Edinger

FAST TIP *40

Paint the Picture

"EVERY NOW AND THEN ONE PAINTS A PICTURE
THAT SEEMS TO HAVE OPENED A DOOR AND SERVES
AS A STEPPING STONE TO OTHER THINGS."
— Pablo Picasso

There is a term in the real estate industry for when an agent massively drops all the terms and names of items included in a home. It's called feature dumping. A large number of real estate professionals "feature dump" while marketing properties or even during showing appointments because they have never learned the art of "painting the picture." It is a skill that will quickly define your success, or lack thereof, in the new-home market. Selling something that is not yet built is virtually impossible if you cannot help prospects visualize what they are considering purchasing.

There is a phrase often used to illustrate the point of "feature dumping" and it is . . . "Features tell and benefits sell." When showing a home, value is not added by simply saying, "And here is the fireplace." In order to effectively use emotions, consider saying, "And here is the 42-inch direct-vent gas fireplace. A direct-vent fireplace provides nice and steady warmth." Then, continue by explaining, "It won't heat you out of the room like a ventless fireplace can do. This enables you to enjoy the ambiance while entertaining friends or just relaxing with family. That sounds wonderful, doesn't it?" Most people have no clue what the differences are between the types of fireplaces and will appreciate you taking the time to explain how this particular fireplace is or is not good for them.

Another example would be: "Mr. and Mrs. Richardson, look at the six-burner gas cooktop in the kitchen" (a feature), versus, "Wouldn't that be great for all the entertaining you mentioned you like to do?" (a benefit with a tie-down).

When thinking about features versus benefits, remember that the definition of buying is emotion backed by logic. Logic makes them *think*. Emotions make them *act*. Features justify a price. Benefits justify a purchase. Building value throughout the process is crucial to the selling process. If you skip the value-building, you will end up taking prospects from home to home and when they finally decide on writing an agreement, it will be low because they will fail to see the value in the price. (See Tip 26 for more on how value affects price.)

FAST TIP *4̶1

Use Powerful Words

"KIND WORDS CAN BE SHORT AND EASY TO SPEAK,
BUT THEIR ECHOES ARE TRULY ENDLESS."
– Mother Teresa

What is the difference between the words "house" and "home"? One is cold and lifeless; the other is warm and welcoming. After all, home is where the heart is—not house is where the heart is. To own a home (not a house) is the "American Dream." Most people don't want to purchase a "lot." They would, however, like to own a "homesite."

It all comes down to your choice of words. Some other examples of positive versus negative words would include: own vs. buy, agreement vs. contract, initial investment vs. down payment, opportunity vs. sell, and foundation vs. slab.

Remember to use "build the dream words" from Tip 29. They paint the picture for the buyer and build value. Yes, words build value. Another way to put it is: You cannot change the price of the home with your words, but you can change the value of the home with your words.

If you are writing low-ball offers, did you build value? Every buyer I have ever met wants to feel that he or she got the best deal possible. However, if a buyer doesn't know what they are getting, they will be unable to truly appreciate the maximum value of a home. Save yourself some time and trouble and begin using powerful words regularly. By doing so, you will drastically eliminate pricing issues.

FAST TIP *42

Set Clear Expectations

"IN LIFE AND IN MOVIES, IT'S A SIMILAR CHALLENGE,
WHERE YOU HAVE EXPECTATIONS, AND YOU END UP IN
SITUATIONS THAT ARE NOT MEETING YOUR EXPECTATIONS."
— Jeff Bridges

Nothing is more frustrating than unmet expectations. Setting proper expectations from the moment you meet a potential client will reduce stress and enable all parties to work together, rather than struggling contentiously through the process. This includes painting a clear picture as to what the buyer or seller can expect from beginning to end.

As I have said for years when speaking and teaching on this very topic, "Not all surprises are good ones." This is a simple lesson I learned early on in my career. Covering what the process entails leaves little room for misunderstandings, thereby leading to higher customer satisfaction that will contribute to the growth of your business through referrals and previous client testimonials.

Having a system in place to ensure that key conversations occur, and subsequent touch points happen throughout the transaction, helps to minimize last-minute mishaps. For example, disclosing homeowner association fees can be easily overlooked. They are frequently a source of last-minute issues, due to an oversight earlier in the process. Almost always the buyers get upset. Not because of the fees, but because they weren't told upfront. The real root of the problem, when something like this happens, is expectations. People want to know what to expect. When omissions are discovered, they can be the breeding ground for mistrust to take place. To avoid issues like this coming up and affecting your success, use checklists of usual important items that need to be covered, like home owners association dues, to ensure important points are covered throughout the process.

FAST TIP *43

Know Your Numbers

While writing this book, I considered how this tip could certainly be merged with a tip or two throughout this book. However, after some consideration, I decided it is just too important to combine—mostly due do to the appallingly large number of seasoned agents who have asked me to calculate property taxes for them to show to their clients. The "seasoned" part that I mentioned shows a need for a higher level of discussion on this topic.

If an agent does not know how to figure a monthly mortgage payment or calculate property taxes, there is no way their clients are making fully informed decisions. Unless, of course, that agent is leaving all the number-crunching up to a mortgage broker and title attorney, which I would not recommend. Don't depend on others to do what you can easily learn to do yourself. To learn how to figure a monthly payment, contact your loan officer alliance partner and ask that he or she teach you the steps to figuring payments. To learn how to calculate property taxes, call the title company that closes your transactions and ask that someone teach you how to figure property taxes for each of the counties and special school districts where you do business. And finally, when all else fails, you can always look up the tax assessor's office on the internet for the county in which you are selling homes, and you will find this information on the county website.

FAST TIP *44

Always Be Closing

"ALWAYS BE CLOSING. THAT DOESN'T MEAN YOU'RE ALWAYS
CLOSING THE DEAL, BUT IT DOES MEAN THAT YOU NEED
TO BE ALWAYS ON THE NEXT STEP IN THE PROCESS."
— Shane Gibson

As a sales professional, you must recognize a vital truth: Many of the steps in the sales process point directly toward "The Close." It is only the final step that does not. That final step *depends* upon the close. This step will be much easier if you hone your closing skills by ABC—"Always Be Closing."

By definition, there should be a number of "closings" within the framework of your planned presentation. There doesn't need to be a big lead up to an ending close. It is an ongoing process of numerous closes so that at the end, it seems only natural to sign an agreement.

Unless you ask for the sale and complete the agreement, you are failing your prospect and yourself. You owe it to them to close them. Statistics show that the majority of sales professionals have a fear of rejection. In fact, years ago, I heard an expression that I have never forgotten, "The fear of rejection can be paralyzing at times." I have always known that phrase would become etched in my memory because I can remember early on in my career feeling completely and utterly paralyzed, sweaty palms and all.

The level of success that you achieve is directly related to how well you can overcome this fear. If your success is being held back because of this, make it a point to become a fearless closer. Personally, I overcame my fear of rejection shortly after identifying the problem, because it was something that I recognized, tackled, and worked hard to remind myself regularly that whatever happens, it's just business—it's not personal.

FAST TIP *45

Ask Involvement Questions

"THE INTERVIEWER MUST BE CURIOUS
ABOUT EVERYTHING."
– Larry King

Successful sales agents are professional communicators. They recognize that asking discovery questions helps them guide prospects toward becoming satisfied customers. Words, when added onto declaratory statements, turn those statements into interrogatory statements, or involvement questions. However, do not use an involvement question unless you are absolutely sure that a reasonable person would have a difficult time saying, "No" to it. For example: When you have a beautiful design feature, such as kitchen cabinets, you would suggest involvement by simply saying, "These cabinets are beautiful, aren't they?"

Involvement questions have the ability to turn features into benefits, which prospects will experience from their frame of reference. When something becomes personal, it then becomes important. The secret is to use questions that bring the prospect closer to an emotional investment.

TWO TYPES OF INVOLVEMENT QUESTIONS

1. CONCLUSION

   When involvement question words are at the end of a statement:
   "This family room is spacious, isn't it?"

2. TAG-ON

   When involvement question words are added onto something
   positive the customer has said:

   Customer: "These hardwood floors are beautiful."

   You: "They are beautiful, aren't they?"

FAST TIP *46
Ask Powerful Questions

"JUDGE A MAN BY HIS QUESTIONS RATHER
THAN BY HIS ANSWERS."
—Voltaire

The most under-utilized strategy for building relationships, getting to know others on a deeper level, and exercising influence, is asking powerful questions. These are questions that are designed to help you engage with others more relevantly and to ensure that you are talking about meaningful issues. Questions uncover what people are passionate about, and may provoke new perspectives on their challenges.

With the correct approach, asking powerful questions can lead to building relationships, winning new business, and influencing others— no matter who you are interacting with. By planning which questions you are going to ask, prior to meeting with prospects, you set the stage for feeling confident by being prepared, and you now have the ability to maximize your time while having face-time with prospects.

Make no mistake—there is an art, if you will, to this question asking. This does not mean you should go about aimlessly asking questions that don't make sense. It means you should know the different types of questions that exist and how they can greatly assist you in connecting with new prospects. When done right, these Q&A

sessions lead not only to increased sales, but also facilitate your ability to provide exceptional service throughout the sales process.

When asking powerful questions of prospects, consider asking about their careers, goals and challenges, passions, and random personal topics such as hobbies and interests.

FAST TIP ✱47

Overcome Objections

"AN OBJECTION IS NOT A REJECTION; IT IS SIMPLY
A REQUEST FOR MORE INFORMATION."
— Bo Bennett

Prospective home-buyer objections are signposts of interest in a home. Let me repeat that. Prospective home-buyer objections point the way and reveal interest in a home. Objections are often hidden requests for more information, and should be treated as such. A person enters a home because of a desire to purchase. The sales professional has a job to reaffirm this desire, reassure the customer's choice in visiting, and instill pride in knowing that he or she will purchase a product of tremendous quality and value.

Here is a six-step process of overcoming a customer's vocalized objection:

STEP 1: HEAR THE OBJECTION OUT.

Far too many sales professionals pounce on the turn-down statement before the prospect gets the words out. Not only does this interrupt and irritate the customer, but it makes the sales professional look pushy and unprofessional.

STEP 2: FEED THE OBJECTION BACK.

This is a critical point that many like to skip—don't skip it. This strategy often helps the prospect answer their own objection as they hear it spoken back. Practice doing this and it will become an automatic response for you.

STEP 3: QUESTION THE OBJECTION.

Ask the prospect to elaborate. Say, "I'm curious," or "Can you elaborate on that?" Ask, "Mr. Jones, what do you mean about the backyard? Do you feel it's too large or too small?"

Be serious and curious. Get to the root of their objection. Often the objection will be removed by the prospect. If not, while the prospect is answering your question, you will have a moment to prepare for their next volley.

STEP 4: ANSWER THE OBJECTION USING YOUR PRE-PLANNED RESPONSES.

Even the best-planned neighborhoods have some weak points. Don't run from strong objections. Use them. You can uncover a gold mine of "hot buttons" in this step if you maintain control while showing sensitivity, warmth, and empathy.

Make a comparative advantage statement: "Mr. Jones, I can understand and appreciate that, and allow me to point out . . ." Without admitting your weakness, you can build your case with stronger features and benefits.

If your prospect accepts your answer, move to step five. If they raise the same objection, go back to steps one through four and pinpoint the exact problem. Then, go on to step five.

STEP 5: CONFIRM THE ANSWER.

Don't overcome the objection and then leave it hanging in mid-air. Even if you were completely clear in your mind, the prospect may not have heard or understood what you covered.

After you answer the objection, confirm the fact with a
concluding tie-down. Ask, "That's the answer you were looking
for, wasn't it?" or "That makes sense, doesn't it?"

If the prospect doesn't understand or doesn't agree, you are
better off knowing right then. If the prospect isn't satisfied,
redefine by going back through steps one through five before
moving ahead.

If the prospect nods or verbally agrees, move on immediately
to the next step.

STEP 6: MOVE ON!

If the objection has been answered satisfactorily, don't wait around
for it to come back to haunt you. Shift gears. Use transition phrases
like, "Oh, by the way . . ." or "Wait until you see this!" The concept
is to avoid getting hung-up on the same objection repeatedly.

FAST TIP *48

Become a Master Negotiator

"DURING A NEGOTIATION, IT WOULD BE WISE NOT
TO TAKE ANYTHING PERSONALLY. IF YOU LEAVE
PERSONALITIES OUT OF IT, YOU WILL BE ABLE TO
SEE OPPORTUNITIES MORE OBJECTIVELY."
— Brian Koslow

Sadly, if few people learn the sales process, even fewer people learn how to negotiate. As real estate professionals, it is your fiduciary responsibility to assist your clients with getting the best deal possible. Without the learned skill of negotiation, it is virtually impossible to fulfill this obligation.

Think of your real estate business as having a toolbox that includes all the tools needed to have a successful career. When you have a tool, you care for it and sharpen it. The negotiation skill is a tool that is sharpened with practice and experience—improving with each newly completed transaction in your toolbox.

Years ago, I showed my brother-in-law, Kevin, and future sister-in law, Kelly, a home that was just perfect for them. They were in love with the home. However, after preparing a comparative market analysis for the home, I explained that the home was clearly overpriced. To complicate matters, the seller had gotten married to the daughter of the Listing Agent. The home had been vacant for quite some time and the seller needed to sell the home quickly. It seemed clear to me that the home showed well and that it had not sold because the home was improperly priced.

After writing an agreement, the Listing Agent presented a counter-offer based on what the seller owed for the property—a common error. I explained the basis for the offer again and advised Kevin and Kelly not to proceed with the home purchase. After waiting for three weeks, I called the Listing Agent to resubmit our offer, reminding her that what her seller owes has nothing to do with what the property was worth. The seller accepted the offer.

Four weeks later, while attending the closing, the seller stood up in front of all parties involved (including his new mother-in-law) and declared, "I just have to shake your hand. You are one heck of a negotiator and next time I sell a home, I want you on *my* side." Everyone laughed, including his new mother-in-law, the Listing Agent.

FAST TIP *49
Follow Up

"THOSE PEOPLE BLESSED WITH THE MOST TALENT DON'T
NECESSARILY OUTPERFORM EVERYONE ELSE. IT'S THE
PEOPLE WITH FOLLOW-THROUGH WHO EXCEL."
— Mary Kay Ash

Following up with leads, prospects, and clients is crucial to the success of your business. Research shows that most prospects do not buy the first time they look. They usually have to encounter a marketing message multiple times before making a purchasing decision. This makes follow-up an essential ingredient in the selling process.

Additionally, the sales process includes conversations that I compare to a tennis match. When you and your clients are about to depart from one another, in person or over the phone, assess the situation and ask yourself: "Whose court is the ball in?" In other words, if they didn't sign an agreement of some sort (listing, purchase, etc.), how are you going to move forward? What is your next strategy? Leave with a reason for *you* to follow up with them. Never put the future of the deal in the customer's hands.

Examples of leaving the next move up to the customer would include them saying, "Well, we are going to go over the information you gave us and get back with you." Or, "After we look everything over, we will call you if we have any questions."

Stop! Hold the presses. Do not pass go. Never do this. Whoever is holding the ball is responsible for the next step. Hear me now: You *must* be holding the ball when you part ways so here are some helpful hints to make sure you're still in the game.

Always have some sort of outstanding issue or reason for a friendly follow-up call. Here are a few examples:

1. "Mr. Jones, I will call right away to find out the average utility expenses. When I get them, I will contact you immediately."
2. "Mr. and Mrs. Smith, I know you mentioned needing to take some time this evening to think about it. Is 8:00 a.m. or 10:00 a.m. tomorrow best for me to call and follow up with you?"
3. "I will be able to find out the estimated completion date of the home you selected by 10:00 a.m. tomorrow morning and will call you as soon as I confirm it."

A study done by the Association of Sales Executives revealed that 81% of all sales happen on or after the fifth time of contact. If you are only doing one or two follow-up calls, imagine all the business you are losing! Not following up with your prospects is the same as filling up your bathtub without first putting the stopper in the drain.

FAST TIP *50

Be Mindful of Buyer's Remorse

"FORGET REGRET, OR LIFE IS YOURS TO MISS."
— Jonathan Larson

Understand that after making a major life decision such as purchasing a home, many people begin to experience doubts or start second-guessing the big decision they just made, which is commonly referred to as "Buyer's Remorse." There are many ways to address it that demonstrate your understanding, while letting them know at the same time that this is a normal feeling and does not mean they made a wrong decision.

First, congratulate them! Remind them that this is an exciting event and a time to be celebrated. After all, it is not every day that one purchases a home. Then, address "Buyer's Remorse" in a funny, albeit caring manner. For example; hand the buyers a prescription bottle filled with M&Ms labeled "Buyer's Remorse Pills." Explain how the various colors are for various symptoms—perhaps blue for fear, yellow for anxiety, etc.

Keep in mind that this tip is not about convincing a buyer to purchase a home that is not right for them. This is about helping your clients get to where they are trying to go. Change can be very nerve-racking for some and no matter how awesome the property, they are going to feel this way and it can be painful but normal.

Many times after completing the new-home agreement, I have said something like this: "How exciting all of this is! Now, look, I know that we have been together making decisions about your new home today. And tonight after you get home, climb into bed, and try to get to sleep, you might say to yourselves, 'Oh goodness! Honey, what have we done?' That is okay. It is normal. It's called Buyer's Remorse." As I grab the Community, Covenants, and Restrictions, I continue on to say, "I have something to help you go to sleep tonight just fine. You see, just begin reading on page one of the Community Restrictions and I am pretty certain you won't make it past page three!"

It has been incredible for me to experience such a low cancellation rate through the years. I attribute that low cancel rate to my acknowledgement of "Buyer's Remorse," sharing that those feelings can be normal, and even joking about it in a kind, understanding, and professional way.

FAST TIP *51

Provide Unparalleled Customer Service

"THE BEST WAY TO FIND YOURSELF IS TO LOSE
YOURSELF IN THE SERVICE OF OTHERS."
— Mahatma Gandhi

Delivering quality customer service is both a responsibility and an opportunity. Too often salespeople view customer service as an administrative burden that takes them away from making a sale. The truth is that providing customer service offers a golden opportunity for cross-selling, up-selling, receiving glowing client testimonial letters, and generating quality referrals.

Customers describe quality customer service in terms of attention to detail and responsiveness. Customer satisfaction surveys consistently point to the fact that little details make a big difference. Not surprisingly, the top two customer complaints with regards to customer service are unreturned phone calls and a failure to keep promises and commitments.

Good customer service should be an expectation. And, depending on the product and the price, you may have higher and lower definitions of what is good. For example, you probably do not have the same expectation at a fast-food restaurant as you would at a fine-dining establishment. You pay more and expect more. You pay less and expect less. A real estate transaction is a pretty high-priced item, so the expectation should be high.

That being said, telling your prospective clients that you pride yourself on your "service," is not a differentiation. It's an expectation. However, pleasing people by going the extra mile is a way to provide a "wow" customer service experience.

Here are three powerful ways to go the extra mile:

1. PAY ATTENTION TO THE SMALL DETAILS.
   Return phone calls, text messages, emails, and other correspondence immediately.

2. STAY IN CONTACT AND KEEP GOOD RECORDS.
   Jot down notes from phone calls and meetings, making certain to record all relevant information.

3. UNDER-PROMISE AND OVER-DELIVER.
   Develop a reputation for reliability; never make a promise that you cannot keep. Your word is your bond.

Successful salespeople develop the habit of always going the extra mile when providing service. Your ability to build a successful sales career is in direct proportion to the quality and quantity of service you render on a daily basis. Want to close more sales and get tons of quality referrals? Begin today to improve your customer service skills by developing the habit of always going the extra mile, or two.

TESTIMONIAL

I have been a civil engineer, contractor, and builder for over twelve years with the majority of that experience specializing in building. Whether buying, selling, or building a home, my experience with and my opinion of real estate agents has never been good. Most agents place your home information on MLS and that's it. They don't think outside the box, work different ideas, and spend the time needed to actually sell a home in today's market. Then I met Michelle.

We met in 2008, on a large-scale development, and from the very beginning, she wanted to be involved in every aspect of the project. She provided a very needed and welcomed opinion full of experience and fresh ideas, due to the knowledge she had gained working with some of the largest development companies in the country.

Later, when I set out to build a high-end home, I knew that we had a great design, but I was unclear on the price point and placement of the home. Furthermore, because of the other businesses I own and run, I was unsure if I even had time to deal with the marketing and customer relations that were required. After taking into account all the obstacles involved, I knew that Michelle was the person I needed to hire.

From the beginning, she reviewed and gave valuable input on my building plans and helped set a price point on the home based on the amenities, the competition, and house comparisons around us, so that not only could I make the margins that I needed, but get showings almost immediately.

I have never met a real estate agent who is more willing to take the time to make a deal work and offer customer service that is frankly, unparalleled. In addition to the fact that she sold a $600,000 house within two months in a down economy, she helped me with my dealings on the contractor/seller side, and (in my opinion) did the buyer's real estate agent job as well.

When it came to flooring, paint, cabinets, electrical, plumbing, and everything else that goes into a home's selection, she was at every meeting for the buyer. She was professional, on time, and for the first time, I felt that a real estate agent earned every penny they were being paid. To put it simply, she made my job easier.

Due to her experiences and God-blessed talent, she is an excellent real estate agent and the standard to which I believe all real estate agents should aspire. After dealing with Michelle, I now know what the normal should be and will never settle for less.

—Joshua Spradlin, Alliance Building Group, LLC

FAST TIP ✳52

Be a Great
Team Player

"TEAMWORK IS WHAT MAKES COMMON PEOPLE
CAPABLE OF UNCOMMON RESULTS."
— Pat Summit

Have you ever met a successful person who has not had support and leadership from another person? A crucial factor when achieving great success in the real estate industry, or any industry for that matter, is teamwork. Unity is a place of power.

Currently, we live in a throw-away culture. I am not just talking about using paper plates, plastic utensils, and red Solo cups. Our society is experiencing higher divorce rates than ever before and parents are leaving behind children at a staggering rate. Living this way produces a great number of casualties, unfortunately. And if you choose to run your business with no loyalty, are quick to replace team members, you will lose momentum and your success will certainly pay the price.

In all real estate transactions, there are many other professionals that are needed to get the deal done. Your needs can include a mortgage broker, home inspector, appraiser, land surveyor, and many more. There are numerous factors to consider when building a team of go-to professionals or, as I like to call them, alliance partners.

First, since sales pros understand they are measured by the

company they keep, they surround themselves with a team of top-notch alliance partners. You know them, they are dependable, they return their calls, they are on time to meetings, they are the best at what they do, and you can vouch for their superior customer service. If they don't run their businesses as professionals, finding someone who does should be an urgent priority.

Second, when considering alliance partner candidates, I have found it critical to the success of the team to clearly define what is expected, and to fully understand what is needed from you. For example, when meeting with a title company, you need to understand what they need from you so that you are never the reason why they are unable to perform their job well. Then, do your part of being a great team player by not only addressing what you need from them but also by tending to what they need from you.

Third, when problems arise, many times it is due to the lack of communication at some point in the process. While keeping the lines of communication open at all times is a necessity, consider implementing a few systems that can ensure every alliance partner has the information needed as quickly as possible. For example, consider having specified weekly or bi-weekly phone conference calls or email update times with certain alliance partners, like the preferred mortgage broker, or by naming a specified way to communicate (text or email) when certain tasks are completed, like when a home inspection or termite inspection is finished.

Ultimately, delivering a one-of-a-kind experience to your clients is the goal. Take an objective look at how you and your team are performing, quickly implement any needed changes, and commit to minimizing turnover in the team.

FAST TIP *53

Collect Client Testimonials and Ask for Referrals

"IF YOU DO BUILD A GREAT EXPERIENCE,
CUSTOMERS TELL EACH OTHER ABOUT THAT.
WORD OF MOUTH IS VERY POWERFUL."
— Jeff Bezos

A successful agent isn't necessarily doing one hundred transactions a year. Today, success is measured by the satisfaction they provide their clients day in and day out. Certainly, a healthy number of transactions is important, but what is more important is that real estate agents measure success by how the client feels at the end of the transaction.

Finding out how clients feel is easy—just ask. By asking, you have the ability to find out what's working and what isn't. It's a report card of just how well you are (or aren't) serving your clients. This is the time to monitor how your clients perceive the quality and quantity of the service you provide. Service is not defined by what you think it is, but rather how your clients perceive its value. When it comes to customer service, perception is most definitely reality.

If they aren't happy about a step in the process, do whatever is possible to right the wrong and use it as a learning curve. And whenever possible, quickly take steps to ensure it does not happen again with future clients. If they are happy, ask for a testimonial letter and for referrals.

Collecting testimonial letters is my favorite strategy, not only because they are freely given, but because they work more effectively than any other strategy I've ever used. In fact, most of the time, these are more important than what you have to say about how you conduct business. You see, most people prefer to avoid unnecessary risk. When prospective clients read or hear the great things people are saying about you, that gives you instant validation. You are a much lower risk in the prospect's mind. By the way, this rings true for referrals as well.

Asking for referrals throughout the process is where the rubber meets the road. A testimonial is one thing—it's passive—however; an active referral is a sign of a very different level of satisfaction and delight with your services. Asking for referrals leads me to contemplate a popular old adage that I have heard many times: "Give a man a fish, he eats for a day. Teach a man to fish, he eats for a lifetime."

I recommend that you put into action a consistent system of asking for referral sales at appropriate times. Strive for at least five referrals from each of your clients by asking, "Who do you know that may be looking to buy or sell a home today that could use my professional real estate services?"

FAST TIP *54

Be Balanced

"IT'S GOOD TO HAVE MONEY AND THE THINGS THAT
MONEY CAN BUY, BUT IT'S GOOD, TOO, TO CHECK
UP ONCE IN A WHILE AND MAKE SURE YOU HAVEN'T
LOST THE THINGS THAT MONEY CAN'T BUY."
—George Horace Lorimer

While we may say that family comes first, so many times the family is always having to sacrifice because Mommy or Daddy has to show this house at the last minute or has to take this call. I know first-hand the allure that the "thrill of the deal" can have, but to achieve real success in life requires you to have the key abilities to self-audit and be honest with yourself.

Does your family really come first? Have you really prioritized them and their needs over your own ambitions? These are not easy questions to ask yourself or answer but they are necessary if you are going to live the full, well-rounded life that you deserve.

It is so important to live, laugh, and love. One way to make family and friends a priority is by making "appointments." Schedule the time to exercise regularly, attend birthday parties, take loved ones to dinner, and go on vacation. Sure, there will be the occasional emergencies that pop up but keep balance in your life to empower you to be the best you can be—whether in business or in your personal life.

While selling homes for a national home builder in 1999, my accomplishments were impressive and plenty; however, my personal life fell apart that year. Every important relationship in my life suffered greatly. I missed date nights with my husband, birthday parties of family members and friends, and even much-needed days off were spent working instead of rejuvenating and taking care of myself and personal affairs.

That year my husband and I built a home that I only went to see two times during the five-month construction process. The custom builder forgot to add the front porch and I was too busy to even check-in to ensure everything was going according to plan. Needless to say, we ended up with a home that had no covering for our visitors while they were at our front door, ringing the doorbell. I know this sounds unbelievable, although I can assure you . . . it is true. I sold nearly one hundred homes that year and failed miserably to take the time to have balance in my own life. A valuable lesson I learned the hard way is that you must always put the oxygen mask on yourself first before you can be of any help to those in your sphere of influence.

Real estate is said to be a 24/7 business, much like any small business. However, in order for you to be at your best for your clients, it is of paramount importance not to lose sight of your personal values including your physical health, and your relationships with family and friends. True balance means taking care of your health so you can enjoy your family and friends, which then leads to an environment that is conducive for experiencing success in your career. Your health, as well as help and understanding from family, is needed to be truly successful in this business.

FAST TIP *55

Have Fun

"WE RARELY SUCCEED AT ANYTHING
UNLESS WE HAVE FUN DOING IT."
— Rev. John Naus

You *can* do what you love and have fun doing it! Yes! I give you permission to do just that, in case you are feeling overwhelmed with trying to juggle it all. While working for a large home builder, I had a Senior Vice President of Sales and Marketing who would always bring up having fun and the importance of "enjoying" selling. Whether it was in a sales meeting or while having an individual conversation with him, he would always find a way to bring up the incredible healing power of simply having fun. Many times, he'd ask, "You're having fun, aren't you?" At the time, I didn't understand it and felt he was even being a bit cheesy. However, looking back on it, I now understand. I also remember another Vice President of Sales and Marketing who devised very unique team-building exercises which included playing "Let's Make a Deal" at the sales meetings. I will never forget how much fun we had with those office games!

When you enjoy what you are doing, everything and everyone benefits. You are excited and passionate about what you do and that excitement and passion shows. When excitement and passion are evident, people want to be around you—including prospects. Prospects will want to do business with you because your joy is contagious.

There's an old saying, "No man ever said on his deathbed I wish I had spent more time at the office." Some of the people you meet along the way that start out as clients and end up as friends truly do make this business fun. They are the heartbeat of your business as you assist them through life's changes . . . so make every day a great day with them, and go out and have a ball!

About the Author

At the age of twenty-three, Michelle Moore was newly married and searching for a career that would compensate her in direct correlation to the hard work and effort she put into it. Since Michelle has never met a stranger, as they say, real estate became the obvious choice.

Her first year in real estate was "on-the-job" training, and she quickly realized that she would either sink or swim by the knowledge she gleaned, the effort she contributed, and the tenacity she mustered. With every "No" she received, she evaluated, studied, and adapted her business model, becoming an avid student to compensate for a lack of experience. She attended training classes and began to learn about personality types, sales techniques, and much more. At the end of her first year as a Realtor®, she was hired by a leading national new-home builder, Beazer Homes, and thus began her fifteen-year career specializing and excelling in new-home construction.

As her knowledge of construction expanded, Michelle applied everything she learned to her business. By the time she was twenty-six, she was an award-winning sales professional in real estate. To date, she has earned over forty sales, leadership, and literary awards which includes earning the National Sales Manager of the Year Award with Zaring Homes by outselling all other agents company-wide in 1999; earning every sales awards given for various accomplishments throughout the year for the entire Nashville Division for Centex Homes in 2002; and by leading a team of six sales professionals to selling 87 homes in less than two weeks in the Lake Providence community in Mt. Juliet, Tennessee, for Pulte Homes in 2006.

Her platform includes training, coaching, inspiring, and motivating thousands of both new-home sales agents and general real estate agents. She passionately challenges agents to "rise to the top" by committing to excellence in all areas of their lives in order to achieve maximum success at the highest level, both professionally and personally. She passionately teaches that coming to hear her speak or teach and reading her books is the easy part. It is step one of a two step process that includes getting the information and the education. But she says, "What good is it if you do nothing with it? Take action! Change your ways so your life, professionally and personally can change too!" She teaches that so many agents don't know what they don't know and says, "Now that you know better, do better!"

Currently she travels the country as an inspirational and motivational speaker, sales trainer, and leadership coach. She is also an award-winning author. *Selling Simplified* received the Bronze Award in Business and Finance books in 2013 by Readers' Favorite. Her personal story and journey from abandonment to forgiveness paves the way for thousands to walk in freedom, as she leads by example around every bend and turn, and is a living testimony to how God makes all of the crooked paths straight.

Michelle is a contributing author in the bestselling book, *God Crazy Freedom*, and is a co-author in the *God Crazy Freedom* mini-book series on *Abandonment to Forgiveness*. Also, she is a contributing author for Nashpreneur.com's book *Ultimate Nashville Business Guide, Women's Edition*.

Michelle lives in Lebanon, Tennessee, with her husband of twenty years, Jeff Moore, and their two sons, Dillon and Carson.

Visit www.BeYourTop.com to connect with Michelle
and find the latest up-to-date information about her
upcoming events and newly released books.

Email Michelle at Michelle@BeYourTop.com to share testimonials
of how the tips listed in her books have helped you to achieve your
goals, and helped you to, as she always likes to say, "Be your top!"

CPSIA information can be obtained at www.ICGtesting.com
Printed in the USA
LVOW04s1126030914

402220LV00002B/2/P